THERE'S NOTHING
WRONG WITH HER

THERE'S NOTHING WRONG WITH HER

A Memoir

M.B. YAKOUBIAN

Full Court Press
Englewood Cliffs, New Jersey

Published in the United States of America
by Full Court Press, 601 Palisade Avenue,
Englewood Cliffs, NJ 07632
fullcourtpress.com

ISBN 978-0-578-88647-3
Library of Congress Control No. 2021912980

*Some names in this book have been changed
for reasons of privacy.*

Cover art by Susan Olinsky (susanolinsky.com)

Cover photograph: andreiuc88/Shutterstock.com

Editing and book design by Barry Sheinkopf

For my dear husband, Dan,
the best person in the world.

ACKNOWLEDGEMENTS

I owe thanks to my extraordinary teachers and my classmates at Gotham Writers, who patiently responded to each chapter. A huge note of gratitude goes to my husband, Dan, and to Bob Gibbons, his Notre Dame classmate and cherished friend, who read every word more than once and provided their insightful criticism. I also need to thank Barry Sheinkopf for his skillful editing and interior design.

This story begins in the year 2000 and ends with my mother's death in 2005. The passage of time since then has not lessened the strangeness of those years or eased the stress I endured. I have documented certain events, hoping to make sense of what happened and possibly offer some insight to others who find themselves in similar circumstances.

There's Nothing Wrong With Her is a memoir. My memories are imperfect; the events I describe are true to the best of my recollection. The motivations of the characters are my opinion, and any conclusions I draw are based upon my personal interactions with them. Some names have been changed, some events have been compressed, and some dialogue has been recreated. There were undoubtedly many noteworthy events and people pertinent to my mother's story of which I am unaware or have forgotten. I apologize to all those who were part of her life but have not been included in this book.

Table of Contents

I

PHONE CALL

N THE LAST WEDNESDAY in October 2001, I was on my way to the Chelsea Deli to pick up something for lunch when my cell phone rang. I didn't recognize the number; it was from Florida.

"This call is for Mary Yakoubian."

"Yes, speaking."

"This is the Florida Department of Children and Families. We have received a complaint against Mary Yakoubian."

"Oh, really? What kind of complaint?" I began to giggle, thinking the call was a gag.

"Is Elise Yakoubian of Lakeland, Florida, your mother?"

"Yes, that's correct"

"A report has been filed stating that you have been

abusing Mrs. Elise Yakoubian, causing her physical and emotional stress."

I broke off mid-giggle. "*What?* Are you *kidding?*" I froze right there in the middle of the sidewalk. The caller's robotic reading of the charge had made me realize it wasn't a gag. I asked her to please repeat the message—I needed to be sure I'd heard right.

After she repeated the message word for word, I had to sit down somewhere. Quickly. I was too stunned to reply for several seconds. The caller was waiting silently while I caught my breath. I asked her who had filed the complaint.

She said, "We are not permitted to reveal the name or names of those filing a report."

I needed to see it in writing; I would deal with it then. I reeled off the information she requested: name, address, phone, relationship to Elise Yakoubian. She said she would put it in the mail. I thanked her.

I'd lost my appetite. I picked myself up and walked slowly back to school, where I still had two more classes to teach that afternoon. I was so distracted that I had trouble thinking about who could have filed such a complaint.

I'd just seen Mom a month earlier at her home in Lakeland. We'd gone shopping together, eaten out, visited friends. She'd been her usual cheerful self the entire ten days I was there. Since Mom didn't drive, she was stuck in the house much of the time. Whenever I visited, each day would be like an adventure for her. She'd ask me at breakfast, "What are we doing today?"

As soon as school got out, I called Mark Dolly, a Florida attorney I'd recently retained to help me with Mom's affairs. He got me to calm down and advised me what had to be done. We first needed to get affidavits from Mom's friends that described my relationship with her and interactions they had witnessed between us. If those weren't sufficient, he would see that a hearing was scheduled at which her friends could appear and testify. After a lengthy discussion with him, and of course dollar signs adding up, I felt more in control.

I took out my address book and started making calls to Florida. My first call was to Anita, one of Mom's best friends at Lakeside Baptist Church. She was appalled when I explained what had happened. She assured me that she, and many other friends, would sign affidavits to vouch for me. Together we compiled a list of people who knew both Mom and me well.

Following up during the next few weeks kept me busy. Mr. Dolly forwarded to me copies of the notarized affidavits he had obtained and submitted.

In the end, the case was settled, closed without question. Nine people verified in writing that Mom and I had a great relationship. They described how she looked forward to my visits, and that we clearly had fun together in whatever activity I had planned for us.

There was one Lakeland acquaintance who I was sure

wouldn't vouch for me: Sherry Baker, Mom's house cleaner. Mom was eighty-five and living alone at that time. Sherry had been helping around the house for about twelve years, having started when Dad was still living. I'm sure she knew I wasn't thrilled with the job she'd been doing lately. In addition to house cleaning every Friday, her responsibilities included driving my mother to the bank, where she would withdraw $150.00 in cash. After the bank trip, she'd drive Mom to the supermarket to shop for her weekly groceries. Out of the $150.00, Mom would pay for the groceries and also pay Sherry $50.00, cash only, for her work.

It had come to my attention that Sherry had lately become a lot chummier with my brother Lenny. Lenny wasn't as involved in my mother's affairs and adopted a *laissez faire* attitude when questions such as house cleaning came up. "Getting by" rather than doing things 100 percent was something Sherry and Lenny had in common. Sherry moved a little further away from me as she moved closer to Lenny. Hers was not an affidavit I expected or needed.

Over the past two years, Lenny and I had both observed Mom's symptoms of dementia become more pronounced. We had talked about possible alternatives concerning her care, but he was unwilling to accept the seriousness of her decline, and we hadn't come to any agreement. By the time those affidavits were signed, sealed, and delivered, I was sure my brother had been responsible for filing the frivolous complaint. After he caused that unnecessary trouble, I wondered how he imagined we could work together to help our mother.

A lawyer by training, he had been frugal to a fault for as long as I could remember. He was well aware that I had been awarded primary power of attorney for handling Mom's affairs. This may have frightened him into believing I would go ahead and pay too much for her care.

The money in the accounts she lived on was entirely her own, left to her by Dad. Maybe Lenny felt it was his future inheritance and didn't trust me to be as economical with Mom's money as he would be. Maybe he was planning some legal finagling to stop me from using my authority to spend on her what I felt was needed.

I had underestimated Lenny. That troublesome phone call was just the beginning.

2

PRELUDE

THE WORLD WAS AT WAR IN 1941; I was an infant, barely one year old. In the U.S., many necessities were in short supply, food staples were rationed, and there was a decline in the number of families who had the means to buy their own homes. Builders were hungry for work, many willing to begin construction with a miniscule down payment if the prospective client had a job and was in a position to make future payments.

My extended family, bursting at the seams of their house in Bridgeport, Connecticut, found just such a builder. The Yakoubian family of five included my grandparents John and Mary, their eldest son, my father, Leon, with his wife, my mother, Elise, and me, their first born. The builder they found needed the work; he had struggled through the Depression, and now the War was taking its toll on the private construction business. Seeing that the hard-working Yakoubians could be trusted, he agreed to build a roomy, two-story home to accommodate us on an acre of land my parents had chosen in neighboring Stratford.

Our white colonial house on a hill was built in record time, with a total price tag of $10,000.00. We five, including my grandparents, whom I called "Nonie" and "Pop," moved into the three-bedroom, two-bathroom house a few months before the birth of my brother Johnny, my parents' second child.

While Stratford is located just seventy-five miles east of New York City, my family—parents and grandparents alike—could still have been living in Aleppo, Syria. They all adhered to prescribed roles, exactly as their parents and grandparents used to do in Turkey and Syria. The men, breadwinners, had jobs while the women stayed home to cook, clean, and care for children.

When my father and his family were living in Syria in the early 1900s, Nonie used to treat her two children, my father and his brother, George, so differently, they could well have been living in two different homes. For some reason, she was cold and strict with my dad, her first son, but doted openly on George, allowing him unfettered freedom. Their personalities as adults reflected this disparity. My dad became timid, obedient, lacking self-confidence; George became loud, aggressive, willing to try anything. Dad followed school rules, graduated high school with honors, and went on to Columbia College of Pharmacy. George dropped out of high school and went to work, picking up a variety of skills on the fly, and made a lot of money.

In July 1920, the four Yakoubians from Aleppo disembarked onto Ellis Island, their names then Zadour, Majida, Levone, and Krikor; they entered the U.S. re-named John, Mary, Leon, and George. They settled in the Bay Ridge section of Brooklyn. At that time, Bay Ridge was the area where many Syrians headed upon entering the U.S.

Dad's family had fled Turkey well before the mass genocide of 1915 and had become more Syrian than Armenian. Leon and George spoke no Armenian at all; the family spoke Arabic with one another and Turkish with other Armenians. Once they settled in Bay Ridge, their olive skin, angular features, dark hair, and short stature made them virtually indistinguishable in appearance from their Syrian Arab neighbors.

Among their few relatives in the U.S., the Yakoubians had a cousin, Hagop, living in Bridgeport, Connecticut. Hagop urged them to move there, where, he believed, there were more opportunities than in New York City. George decided to follow Hagop's advice, whereupon my grandmother picked up the rest of the family to follow him there. The uprooted family moved into a wood frame house on Jewett Avenue in Bridgeport.

In short order, with the backing of Hagop, George opened two small grocery stores, similar to today's bodegas—one for my grandfather to operate in Bridgeport, and one for himself in Stratford. On the side, he repaired radios and managed to acquire the skills of a dental technician; Uncle George made the best false teeth in town. He continued to add to his skills, moving into the field of construction work. Within a few years, George had progressed from small handyman jobs to building houses and eventually a strip mall in Stratford. In 1937, he fell in love with Anna, whom he had met in the Italian community near Jewett Avenue. They were married despite the intense objections of my grandmother.

During the same period of time, since Leon (my dad) was unable to immediately find a pharmacist position in town, he worked on an assembly line at Bridgeport Brass, a local manufacturing plant. Two years after George was married, my grandmother pressured him to bend to her wishes and marry Elise Souroghlian (my mom).

The Souroghlian family in Syria consisted of my mother, Elise, and her widowed mother, Arousiag. Although her mother was alive and well, my mom still had to live in an Aleppo orphanage. She was born in 1913 in Diyarbekir, in eastern Turkey, an area which was once part of Armenia. She could barely remember her father, Ohannes Souroghlian, who had been assassinated by the Turks. She and her mother miraculously survived the 1915 "death march" to Syria, though her infant brother perished along the way. Around the same time that she and my grandmother reached Aleppo, the wife of the orphanage director there, Rev. Aharon Shirajian, died of typhus. Since Mom's mother had a college education and proved to be a good worker in the orphanage, Rev. Shirajian agreed she would be a desirable person for him to marry and fill the role of assistant formerly filled by his late wife. I don't understand how marriages were arranged then, especially in that environment, but I believe the woman in question had little to say about the arrangement. Two years after settling in Aleppo, my grandmother was married to Rev. Shirajian.

It turned out there was a great deal of work involved in running the orphanage. Since Arousiag therefore didn't have much time to care for a child, her sister took on the responsibility of looking after my mother. Little Elise admired her mother's tireless devotion to the work, but she saw precious little of her during those years at the orphanage. My mom's needs were met, but an aunt is not quite the same as a mother. I'm convinced that the lack of adequate mothering must have had an adverse effect on her development.

Arousiag and Aharon Shirajian had two children together, Ara and Aranoush. Mom always spoke affectionately of her half-siblings, eight and ten years younger, and has recounted stories about what she remembered as having been a happy family life. Thanks to Rev. Shirajian's stewardship, the thousands of children who passed through the orphanage had adequate food, education, recreation, even music lessons.

There exist a few photos from that time showing my mother as a child, standing unsmiling in the front row among various members of the Shirajian family. One well-preserved photo depicts Elise at the age of eight as a sweet-faced, delicate child, with long wavy hair spread over her shoulders. I've seen only one photo of Mom as a young adult, probably taken a couple of years before her leaving Syria for the U.S. It's a happy, candid photo of my beautiful twenty-something Mom standing alongside her mother, and at their feet are her playful, giggling half-brother and half-sister, Ara and Aranoush, aged about ten and twelve. Mom is wearing a printed cotton dress, and her dark hair is pulled neatly back in a long braid.

Mom was fortunate to have several relatives already living in the U.S. In 1937, her cousins in Providence, Rhode Island, acted as sponsors to bring her to the States; she then lived with them for two years.

There was a sizeable Armenian community in Providence, the religious affiliation of the majority of them being Armenian Orthodox. While all Armenians are Christian, there exist substantial differences between the Orthodox and Protestant Armenians. Critically important to my mother was the fact that her family was Protestant; it was imperative that she, a pastor's daughter, be married to a protestant. Her relatives in Rhode Island proceeded to initiate talks with mutual acquaintances of the Protestant Yakoubians in Connecticut; it was ultimately determined that Leon and Elise would make a good match. My mother was twenty-six, and my father was thirty-two when they married in 1939.

My parents lived with Nonie and Pop on Jewett Avenue in Bridgeport for their first two years together. After I, baby Mary Elizabeth, arrived in 1940, they realized they needed to move to larger quarters. Dad and my grandparents pooled their savings for the down payment on a house to be built to their specifications.

We five Yakoubians moved into the stately colonial in Stratford in 1941. Dad found a suitable Protestant church nearby to attend on Sundays, though for four years, till I reached school age, no one in the family associated with a single one of our neighbors. All were Roman Catholic.

While immigrants to the U.S. often maintain the traditions of their country of origin, my family was even more insular than most other Syrian Armenian émigrés. My grandmother was a domineering woman who acted as the family taskmaster. Nonie's appearance wasn't particularly impressive—average height and on the heavy side—but there was absolutely no doubt who was the boss in the family. Her iron rule had an intensely repressive effect on my mother.

Mom had never lived on her own. She had stepped off the *Queen Mary* in 1937 and, after being closeted for two years in Providence, married by arrangement to Leon. Docile by nature, she meekly followed her mother-in-law's orders to spend the entire day doing housework. The only time Mom was allowed to leave the four walls of the house was to attend church on Sunday. My ultra-religious grandmother did not permit Mom to engage in any "sinful" pastimes such as listening to the radio or reading magazines. She even limited Mom's interaction with us children, as she believed doing anything besides feeding or dressing children was frivolous, a waste of precious time. It wasn't till 1951, when my grandparents had moved out into another house they built right next door, that Nonie's day-to-day micromanaging finally decreased.

Despite all the daily chores my mother had to complete, she still made time to teach me skills that I've carried with me to this day. She taught me to sew when I was eleven years old, in the sixth grade. I learned to make dresses using commercial patterns, and skirts and tops without a pattern. The fashion for girls then was huge skirts worn over layers of ruffly crinoline slips. Fabric was inexpensive in the '50s. Using the skills I learned from my mom, I was able to stitch up the fullest skirt for about $2.00.

In 1957, after both grandparents had passed away, my mother gained the freedom to organize her own time. Unhappily, the period from 1957 to 1977 did not turn out to be particularly carefree for her and my dad. They had never quite recovered from the loss of little Johnny in 1948 at the age of six, the result of a botched surgery. Not wishing to appear harsh, my parents were reluctant to exert any control over the two children they had afterwards, my brothers David and Lenny. They believed David, born in 1949, to be God's replacement for their lost Johnny. And the God-given role for Lenny, born in 1951, was to be a playmate for David. Neither Mom nor Dad had developed as a strong parent, and neither provided much in the way of discipline. They were gentle, compliant people, overwhelmed by their two undisciplined young boys who had become, by the 1960s, unruly adolescents immersed in the drug culture.

As often happens with arranged marriages, my mom and dad grew to love one another deeply. They were dutiful, religious people who wanted to always do the "right thing," as they'd been taught. However, this gentle couple were not well prepared to raise children. They apparently expected that, once the children came into the world, they would naturally be as obedient and compliant as their parents had been.

Mom and Dad believed that, if they gave David everything he wanted and free rein to do whatever he pleased, he would be a perfect, happy child. They neglected to give him what he really needed: a knowledge of his boundaries. His behavior mystified them. The older he got, the more vehemently he demanded defined limits, and the more confused our parents became. He was frustrated in his interactions with others, who didn't pander to him as his parents did. By the time he reached adolescence, he was utterly out of control, unhappy, and acting out impulsively. David was ready for the immediate gratification offered by drugs.

Young Lenny observed his older brother's outbursts and found more effective methods for getting his way. He became adept at nagging, whining, and pestering—he'd just tug relentlessly at Mom's hem till she gave in. Lenny grew to be a fast talker who wouldn't give up—he'd just talk and talk a blue streak till Mom or Dad caved in out of self-preservation.

An example of Lenny's manipulative behavior was displayed a few months after high school. He had begun attending Quinnipiac College in Hamden, a school that, in those days, would accept just about anyone who paid the tuition. At that stage in Lenny's life, doing drugs took priority over studies. He found the college dorm too restrictive for his activities, so he and some other guys with similar interests found a nearby house they could rent instead. Lenny nagged Mom for days, inventing all sorts of plausible reasons why she should get in the car, go to Hamden with him, and sign papers giving him permission to move into the off-campus house. She complied; he got his way. He also flunked out and wound up in serious legal trouble for dealing drugs. I saw this incident as an early step in Lenny's development as a con man, talented at getting what he wanted through the art of harangue.

Lenny was lucky: instead of sentencing him to time in jail, the State of Connecticut offered him the option of entering a residential drug rehab facility. The highly structured Renaissance House program was crucial in helping him change his life. Following his release two years later, he went on to attend Fairfield University and then American University Law School. Lenny was cut out to be a lawyer.

David, on the other hand, didn't fare well. He had a creative streak and had acquired the skills to work as a professional photographer. Sadly, he was unable to stay off drugs and therefore repeatedly wound up broke.

I was already out of the house and living in Manhattan when David and Lenny were still in middle school, so my awareness of the goings-on in Connecticut was limited to telephone calls with Mom and monthly visits to Stratford.

I didn't entirely avoid the adverse effects of growing up with permissive parents, though my problems didn't approach the seriousness of my brothers'. I believe my luck may be accounted for by the gap in our ages. As a girl coming of age in the innocent '50s, it was a starkly different world for me than it was for boys in the druggy '60s. Once I was settled on my own in New York City, it was a chore for me to work and attend school part time. It took me twice as long, but I eventually earned the degrees and certification required to teach in the New York City public school system. I had to overcome undisciplined study habits, an easier fix than having to deal with addiction to drugs.

In 1977, after my dad had retired from a thirty-year career as a Walgreens pharmacist, and we children grown and gone, the idea of moving started to make sense to him. Some of my parents' Armenian friends, who had already moved south, persuaded Mom and Dad that their savings would go farther in sunny Lakeland, Florida. They went ahead and bought a three-bedroom ranch-style house there, where they would spend their happiest years making new friends, my mother blossoming like a flower.

I need to stress how unworldly my mother still was, even when they moved to Florida. She had lived a dependent life for so many years that it was difficult for her to change. Her daily activities in Connecticut had been primarily limited to housework and, since she had never learned to drive, she was dependent on Dad to take her everywhere. She wasn't even sure of the cost of basic goods, since she never went food shopping. During the time my grandmother lived in the same house with my parents, Nonie had taken charge of making shopping lists. After Nonie and Pop moved next door, my mother had learned to draw up her own lists, but she herself still didn't go to the market. My father would take her list and bring home what she needed. Her information about such things as current events, music, and clothing styles was minimal as well, as most of her interactions outside the house had been on Sundays with members of Bethany Alliance Church. In light of Mom's restricted life in Connecticut, it was gratifying for me to see how liberating the move to Florida became for her.

Once they had resolved to move to Lakeland in 1977, they had to make an important decision—which house to choose: by a lake, or not by a lake. Dad was enchanted with the idea of living in a house by the water in that city of many attractive lakes. The idea so captivated him that when he took Mom house-hunting, they looked primarily at houses that fronted on one of the lakes. Mom, subservient as always, agreed with him a hundred percent of the time. She later admitted to me that she was not keen on the lakefront idea but would never mention her ambivalence to him. She was happy enough that they were leaving Stratford behind, especially because of the difficulties there with my brother David. She had high hopes that they would begin a fresh, new phase in their lives—it felt to her like an adventure, one which she had never before been able to have.

Dad had been extremely frugal during his entire life. Regardless of the size of his income, he'd consistently managed to put away some savings for the future. In this respect, he was like many people who lived through the Great Depression. No matter how much time has passed or how comfortable they have become financially, they are never able to shake off the fear that another depression may be around the corner. So they pinch every penny as if it's their last.

Pharmacists did not earn a whole lot in the '50s and

'60s. Dad had regularly worked two jobs ever since the late 1940s, one full time at Walgreens in downtown Bridgeport, and another part time at a smaller drug store in Stratford. He had, little by little, put money away in "safe" investments, which may not have grown wildly but did grow, so that by the time he retired, he had accumulated a fair-sized nest egg.

Mom and Dad had some long-time friends from Connecticut, the Cholakians, Kazarians, and Hazians, who had settled in Lakeland earlier in the 1970s. Once my parents made the decision to move to the same city, their friends offered plenty of advice to help them boil down their house choices to two finalists, one by a lake and one inland. Dad was close to settling on the lake-front house when suddenly, without explanation, he chose the one inland. He never discussed his rationale with Mom, but she was pretty sure she had figured it out: for about the same amount of money—$50,000—you could get a larger and better-built house, but no lake, inland. She was relieved.

They sold the Stratford property for $65,000, allowing them a cool $15,000 to pay for moving and then decorating the Lakeland house. Within six months, they had painted and completely furnished their new home at 1721 Sylvester Road. They began attending the First Alliance Church, but a year later switched to Lakeside Baptist Church.

Lakeside was the best thing that ever happened to my parents; the congregation there greeted them with open arms. Although the teachings of those two churches was nearly identical, the Baptists were a more upbeat, accepting group. Before long, Mom and Dad started participating in the church's weekday activities. I have an adorable photo of them dressed in makeshift costumes and acting in a play—yes, my shy dad, too—and they're laughing their heads off. Mom and Dad loved their new lifestyle. They became more gregarious and made many friends through the church, whom they frequently visited and entertained at home as well. My parents finally became "Americanized."

3

LAKELAND

It was a sunny March afternoon in 1977, and the movers had just finished carrying in the house-load of furniture hauled by truck from Stratford to Lakeland. "Here—go ahead and buy yourself some lunch," Dad told the two moving men as he handed one a five-dollar bill. He honestly thought he was being generous, giving away money over and above the billed amount for the move. He wasn't aware of the commonly accepted rate of tipping for service workers—waiters, delivery people, baggage porters—as my parents' frugal lifestyle rarely required such services. They did not dine out, traveled only by car, and rarely shopped for items they couldn't bring home in the car. They had lived in their own house in Stratford for thirty-six years, expenses always paid up to date on my dad's pharmacist salary. They had managed to live comfortably and raise three children by watching every single penny. So an optional five-dollar "gift" was indeed reckless.

The movers graciously thanked Dad for the tip and drove off. By then the moving men had had a number of interactions with my parents. They had surely observed that the late-middle-aged Yakoubians were not a wealthy couple accustomed to moving from one state to another. Even the quality of the furniture being transported, sturdy but not extravagant, must have given them a clue as to my parents' means. So they didn't display any consternation at the meagre tip Dad proffered; they thanked him, wished my parents well, and went on their way. Mom sounded excited and happy when she later described that moment to me. I could just picture her standing off to one side, assuming her traditional role of housewife as the men took care of their business.

Lakeland, in central Florida, has a population of around 45,000, located on Interstate 4 midway between Tampa and Orlando. Mom and Dad were ecstatic; they'd made it to Lakeland. Mom was close to tears, hardly believing their good fortune at finding such an attractive, well-maintained house in an equally well-maintained neighborhood. They had arrived by car a day earlier and stayed overnight with their friends the Kazarians.

Ann and Antranig Kazarian had moved to Lakeland a year before my parents and had bought a two-bedroom home not far from Mom and Dad's new place on Sylvester Road. Mom wanted to call Ann right away to let her know their belongings had arrived safe and sound.

The Kazarians were a soft-spoken Armenian couple who had lived in Norwalk, Connecticut, a few miles from my parents in Stratford. They were the same age as Mom and Dad and belonged to the same Protestant religious denomination. Mom credited Ann's calming influence for helping her maintain a low stress level over the turmoil of moving. Ann's disciplined childhood in a Near East Relief orphanage in Ottoman Turkey had made her a strong, self-sufficient person, whom Mom admired.

After spending the night at the Kazarians, Mom and Dad planned to move right into their new home. The movers had placed the bedroom furniture where Mom and Dad directed, and had the living room furniture arranged in a semi-circle in the spacious front room. There was a smaller dining room opening directly off the living room, with just enough space to accommodate their dining set.

Mom was grateful for the sensible room layout, all on one floor—no more stairs to climb to get to the bedrooms. Her favorite feature of the house was the lanai, which enclosed tropical fern and palm trees bordering a seating area and wet bar. A ubiquitous Florida feature, the lanai is a hybrid of screened-in porch and sun room.

Mom was ready to get right to work—make up the bed and set out towels in the master bath. But she first wanted to check in with Ann, eager to tell her about how efficiently the move had worked out. They chatted for a few minutes;

then Ann suggested she and Antranig bring over some pizza for dinner. Mom and Dad were delighted; they felt at home in no time at all. So went my parents first day at their new home in Lakeland.

After settling in, their first order of business was to find an evangelical Protestant church of the same denomination as theirs had been in Stratford. The pastor's wife at Bethany Christian and Missionary Alliance Church in Stratford had acquaintances in Lakeland who were members of the First Alliance Church there. Armed with the information she'd given them, my parents were able to attend and be welcomed on their very first Sunday.

In the area of Connecticut where I used to live with my parents, evangelicals were a minority. Most of our neighbors had been Catholic, the others being "modern" Protestants (the kind who were allowed to dance, go to movies, and drink alcohol). To Mom and Dad's surprise, they found that the majority of their Lakeland neighbors were, like them, evangelical Protestants, predominantly Baptist. Since their faith played such a central role in their lives, this new religious demographic proved to be a plus in speedily adapting to their new home.

My parents made an adventure out of exploring their new neighborhood. They found a Publix supermarket and a Beall's discount clothing store in a nearby mall, and a Florida First Bank across the street. Mom and Dad were having a great time enjoying the balmy weather and trying out all the new places around town.

They did things together and became a more cohesive couple than they had ever been in the past. One of my favorite recollections of their first year there was Mom calling me, bubbling over with laughter, describing in detail how they would load the car with plastic gallon jugs and drive twenty-five miles to Zephyrhills. There they would fill up the jugs with spring water, which was drinkable, unlike the phosphate-tainted tap water in Lakeland, and cheaper than buying water at the supermarket.

Just one year after moving in, Mom and Dad made their most momentous change: they switched churches. This change had the most profound effect on their lives, even more than the move itself. In 1978, one of their neighbors invited them to a special event at her church, Lakeside Baptist. Following the event, several long tables of food and drink had been laid out in the church's annex for the guests. Mom and Dad found the Lakeside crowd a lively, outgoing group. Among the people my parents met were members of the church's outreach committee, who took down their address and phone information. Within the week, they began to receive notices in the mail from Lakeside, inviting them to their services and classes. The following Sunday morning, they chose to attend Lakeside "just for a change."

It didn't take long for them to make the decision to switch permanently.

Mom used to tell me how she sometimes felt embarrassed to be the center of attention during Sunday School class at Lakeside. The born-and-bred Southerners there were fascinated by her history in Turkey and Syria. My parents were the first couple at Lakeside who had survived the Armenian genocide and grown up in the Middle East The pastor even asked Mom to repeat her story at one of the church's multi-cultural events.

The story she told began in 1915, when she was not quite three years old. During the Turkish expulsion of Armenians, Mom hazily remembers walking and walking beside her mother until they finally reached their Aleppo destination. All she would recall was her relentless grip on her mother's skirt the entire time, never letting go even when her infant brother died in their mother's arms and had to be left under a tree. There weren't many other survivors of the death march; it's believed that more than half the Armenians "deported" from Turkey in that march perished in the desert along the way. During World War I, nearly 2,000,000 Armenians were systematically murdered by the Ottoman Turkish government.

Mom lived in Syria from the age of three to twenty-five, when she emigrated to the U.S. I regret not recording her narrative of her life there in Aleppo—it would have made a great book.

At Lakeside Baptist, the members, including seniors, were assigned to Sunday School classes according to their age and sex. The majority of congregants participated in the classes, held an hour before the 11:00 Sunday morning service. Through these smaller homogeneous classes, members formed close friendships, bonding together. Mom and Dad loved their Sunday School classes, finding them upbeat, almost a party atmosphere, and quite different from what they had known at their former church. They fit right in; they were absolutely having fun.

They made the church transition smoothly; each year they became increasingly involved in Lakeside's activities. There were craft classes that Mom attended, numerous youth team-sports events to watch, movies, and other special events followed by a potluck meal in the dining hall. There were also out-of-town day trips where buses were hired to transport everyone. My parents had not had such opportunities in the past; Mom used to call me, even after a long tiring day, to tell me what a good time they had. Lakeside was the best thing that ever happened to them, and their timing was fortuitous—the church's glory days would not last forever.

My parents were quick to adapt their home decorating to a lighter Florida style. Before they moved there, it was obvious to anyone visiting the house that the previous owners, the Ervins, had a preference for red and white. The first thing that caught the eye when approaching 1721 Sylvester was its vivid crimson front door. Elizabeth Arden would have been envious! The entrance led into a small foyer that opened into a spacious living room whose walls were entirely covered in red-and-white flocked wallpaper. The Ervins had also had a concert grand piano, painted glossy white, smack in the center of the room's rear wall. Flanking the gleaming Steinway, modern red and white furnishings sat ensconced in the shaggy white nap of wall-to-wall carpeting.

Floor-to-ceiling red and white was not exactly the color scheme my parents were likely to choose; light neutrals were closer to what they had in mind. By the end of their first year there, they had transformed the interior to their liking. They had the wallpaper stripped and the walls painted a neutral ivory. The new carpeting they chose was a medium beige, its nap not quite as deep as the one it replaced. I'm glad I saw the place as it had looked when Mom and Dad first moved in so I could appreciate what an improvement they made.

Among the additions that made their home distinctive were the treasured pieces of needlework Mom had acquired from the "old country." These were hand-made wall hangings and decorative pillow-covers, all one of a kind, that transformed their place and made it special.

Mom and Dad soon established a regular routine for themselves. They ventured out several times a week, encouraged by the consistently good weather. A common part of Dad's routine at home included leaning back in his recliner and reading the local newspaper; Mom's included a daily phone call with Ann Kazarian. She used to call Ann every single evening at 7:00 p.m.—they would gab for a good hour.

I went to see my parents during Spring break and Christmas vacation, and made longer visits during the summer. I found that all the indoor places in town were air-conditioned; otherwise, the summer heat would have been oppressive. My husband, Dan, and my brothers, Lenny and David, would be there too during Christmas. We could count on Mom having huge quantities of food prepared in advance. The only downer was David's occasional absence because of drug-related issues. Part of the reason Mom and Dad had decided to move was to put distance between them and David, whose addiction-induced behavior was often unbearable.

In addition to visits by their children, Mom and Dad occasionally had other out-of-town guests over the years. Bob Yakoubian, a cousin on Dad's side, visited from Stratford at least once a year. He and his wife and daughter went to Florida together for their annual trek to Disneyland in Orlando. While they were staying at my parents', Bob, who was skilled at handyman work, helped them with odd jobs around the house.

Another regular visitor was Rita Yeretsian-Marcotte, a cousin from Rhode Island on Mom's side. She, along with her two young children and sometimes her husband, stayed over at my parents', then drove each day to Disneyland. A convenient hotel!

In 1985, they had a visitor who stayed with them for a longer period of time. One morning that year, I had dialed my parents' just for a chat. Expecting Mom to pick up as usual, I was surprised to hear a young-sounding voice I didn't recognize.

"Yakoubian residence."

"Okay, hi. Is my Mom home?"

"I'm sorry, Mr. and Mrs. Yakoubian are out. Would you like to leave a message?"

"Uh—do I know you?"

"This is Diane McMoore. I don't think we've met. Who's calling, please?"

"Okay, hi, Diane. This is Mary Beth Yakoubian. You're visiting my parents?"

"Oh, they didn't tell you about me? I'm staying here temporarily. Maybe you know my mother, Mary McMoore."

"Hmmm. Doesn't ring a bell. How do you know my parents?"

"Mr. and Mrs. Yakoubian were members of my grand-father's church in Connecticut. They were friends with my mother; her name was Roe before she was married."

"Oh! Of course! You're Mary's daughter. So what are you doing in Lakeland?"

Diane went on to describe the sudden breakup with her husband. They had been living in the central Florida area; stranded, she desperately needed someplace where she could regroup, and find a job and an apartment. Diane's mother had known my parents for years back in Connecticut and was aware of their relocating. She called them with an urgent request for help. They readily agreed to have Diane stay in their guest bedroom, which had its own adjoining bathroom.

"So, Diane, how are you doing? Are you feeling pretty safe now?"

"I'm fine, really. Your parents are so sweet. Your mother is going to make me fat with all the yummy food she cooks."

"Hah! I know what you mean. It takes me a couple of weeks to recover whenever I get back home from Lakeland. Tell me, how's Mary, your mom? I haven't seen her since she left Connecticut. We'd heard she was divorced some time ago."

Diane told me how her father had cheated on Mary and then left her to marry one of his students at the school where he taught. Diane had reconciled with him, and he acknowledged that he had "done Mary wrong" and was sorry.

Diane McMoore stayed with my parents for a few months and eventually found a job and a small apartment close to Tampa. Mom and Dad were always ready and willing to give a helping hand to someone in need. Over the years, they offered the use of their guest room to others in crisis situations: golden rule people.

In addition to church activities, my parents' social life included the Kazarians and the other two Armenian families who had moved from Connecticut around the same time. Because of their unique shared background, Mom's friendship with her Armenian lady-friends was quite different from her friendship with her "American" friends in the church. Those three families, like Mom and Dad, were immigrants to the U.S., and they normally spoke Armenian when together, their first language.

Mom especially admired Ann Kazarian for her self-confidence. Her husband had passed away in 1987, leaving Ann to fend for herself. Like my Mom, she didn't drive, but she wisely learned how to negotiate the Lakeland Handi-Bus service. Ann would schedule her shopping and lunch dates in advance, then make the necessary appointments to meet the Handi-Bus where and when she needed a ride.

Ann had a heart condition that could sometimes cause her to collapse. Whenever she felt an attack coming on, she would dial EMS and have an ambulance take her to the hospital. Mom used to call and tell me all about Ann getting herself to the ER—I could hear in her voice how she was in awe of her friend's resourcefulness. I understood her admiration of Ann's independence, but I felt badly that Mom had never had the opportunity to develop the confidence to get around on her own.

In the late 1980s, another Armenian family turned up

in Lakeland. The Haroutians, however, were not Mom and Dad's variety of Armenian. Among the Armenians of the world, the language is spoken in two distinct dialects, known as Western and Eastern Armenian. Those who trace their origin to ancient Armenia (now the eastern half of Turkey) speak Western Armenian. Those who come from modern-day Armenia speak Eastern Armenian.

Since our family originated in Turkey, we are Western Armenian. The newcomers to Lakeland, who came from Armenia, were Eastern Armenian. And, like many immigrating to the U.S. from Armenia, they had first paused in Canada before moving on to Glendale, California. Some of the California Armenians don't have a great reputation, thought to be small-time mobsters and portrayed in movies as the "Armenian Mafia."

The Haroutians—parents and three children—moved to Lakeland from Glendale; they were a family of jewelers.

The first thing the father, Harout Haroutian, did was to contact my parents. We never figured out how they found Mom and Dad in a town with few Armenians. My parents were pleased to learn that an Armenian family was moving to Lakeland, even though the language was not exactly the same. Mom was able to understand their dialect and managed to communicate with them adequately; Dad had never learned Armenian at all, but his Arabic dialect was close enough to Harout's to get by.

The second thing Harout did was ask my Dad for

money. He wanted to borrow $25,000.00 in order to open a jewelry store. Dad said no. Though Armenians are supposed to help each other, he didn't know Harout from a hole in the wall. And he had never in his life put money into risky investments.

Harout eventually gave up his quest to get money out of Dad. He apparently got the money from somewhere else, because he opened, not one, but two jewelry stores, one in the Grove Park Mall and one in the Lakeland Square Mall. By their third year in Lakeland, the Haroutians had bought a plot of several acres at the northern end of town and built three houses on the property. The middle one resembled a plantation house, accessed by a circular driveway which in turn sprouted two semi-circular drives leading to the two smaller "children's" houses. Row upon row of lemon trees bloomed behind the houses. An enormous multi-tiered fountain stood at the main entrance; the approach street was re-named Haroutian Court.

The Haroutian sons, dressed alike in spiffy sharkskin suits, worked in the two jewelry stores. Mom and I would drop by one of their stores to say hello when we happened to be out shopping; we rarely saw any customers in either store. The sons told us that their father's expertise was diamond cutting, and that he was in the other store, working "in the back." Whenever Mom called me, she would invariably relate a new Haroutian story. She thought it was hilarious when Harout got the mayor to hold a ribbon-cutting ceremony when they opened the second store. She even sent me the article that had appeared in the *Lakeland Ledger*.

It's true that Dad wasn't as stressed as he used to be over spending his hard-earned money. But he still had a way to go when it came to deciding if something was a necessary expenditure. When I was visiting, we would all go out to a local restaurant for dinner, but Mom and Dad rarely did so when I wasn't there. Dad figured, why spend money unnecessarily when Mom could cook more cheaply? I neglected to suggest to Dad that he might place greater value on Mom's labor—I hoped he would eventually figure that out for himself.

A helpful thing I did on my own was get Mom a clothes dryer. One Christmas when they had already been living in Lakeland for a few years, I saw they still didn't have a dryer. Just as she used to do in Connecticut, Mom would take the laundry out of the washer and lug the basket out to the back yard, where she hung everything on a clothesline. When I suggested to Dad in the past that he buy a dryer, he had replied that Mom didn't need one. I kept my mouth shut and went to Sears and bought her one. I calculated the timing in advance so that it could be installed while I was still in town. That was probably the number-one best gift I ever got for Mom—she couldn't stop thanking me. There was no need to annoy Dad, so I said as little as possible about it, chalking it up as a Christmas present. I really can't blame him; he had managed to build a comfortable home for our family by means of a lifetime of being super-frugal. In the past, in Connecticut, every single purchase had to pass his stringent "necessity" test, and it wasn't easy for him to change.

In 1986, Dan and I weren't married yet, though we'd been living together in Manhattan for four years. That year, both his parents and mine began ramping up their subtle hints, wondering when we might consider getting married. All our siblings had already been married one or more times. Our mothers weren't quite sure how to introduce us to others—"boyfriend" and "girlfriend" seemed too youthful, "fiancé" was not true, "partner" was not in vogue at the time.

We figured it was about time.

We planned a summer wedding in August 1987 near Dan's parents' home in Havertown, Pennsylvania. We decided to have a small private celebration, just parents, in the chapel of the Armenian Protestant Church there, then later a big party in the rec room of the nearby Armenian Catholic Church. My mom and dad would be visiting up north in Connecticut for a few weeks, as they did most summers; it was an easy drive from there to Havertown. Our out-of-town guests would stay overnight at a hotel nearby.

Our wedding reception was a casual affair, with lots of Armenian food and music, that extended over to the next day in the Cox parents' backyard. Neither of our mothers could understand why I chose not to change my last name, as all women used to do in their day. I joked that we were going to be very modern and would both change our names, maybe to Souroghlian. Nobody thought it was a very funny idea. Too bad—there are no Souroghlians in the world.

Dad suffered his first stroke in 1988. It wasn't a deadly serious stroke, but severe enough to limit some of his activities. He probably should have cut down on his driving, too. One afternoon, Mom and Dad had just gotten into the car, which was parked in the garage as usual. He would normally back up about twenty feet, turn right, and follow the short driveway out onto Sylvester Road. That day, they were seated and belted in the car, ready to drive to the supermarket. All of a sudden, the car shot forward, crashed through the garage wall and finally stopped with the entire front half of the car protruding into the side yard.

We later concluded that Dad had suffered another stroke and reflexively extended his leg, slamming on the gas before he was ready to switch gears into reverse. But it happened so quickly, neither of my parents was able to remember it clearly. All they knew later was, one minute everything was normal, and the next minute the car was through the wall. Miraculously, neither Mom nor Dad were injured, and the car was only slightly damaged.

After his first stroke, Dad had a physical therapist come to the house twice a week, and he did make some improvement. Mom liked talking with Scott, the therapist, and pre-pared lunch for him each time he was over for Dad's ther-apy.

Their talks turned to the topic of driving and, after the garage-crash incident, Scott agreed to teach her how to drive. After a few months of lessons, Mom passed her driv-ing test. But she was afraid to drive alone. The first time I visited Florida after she got her license, I tried to get her to go out for a drive. After repeated assurances, the two of us got in the car. She drove around the block; it was scary. I could see she wasn't sure what to do next—step on gas, step on brake, steer right or left. Fortunately, only a few other cars were on the road. I don't know how she ever passed the driving test, but she definitely needed more practice. By that time, Dad's therapy sessions had been discontinued, so Scott was no longer around to help her.

My brother Lenny and I talked on the phone about our parents' tenuous situation. We agreed that Mom had her hands full, and that they needed to hire someone to help her around the house at least once a week. Dad's driving ability wasn't improving either; I felt they needed someone who would be able to take Mom to the supermarket as well. Lenny assured me that wasn't necessary—Mom had a license and could drive herself. I objected to that idea, describing to Lenny how uncomfortable she was behind the wheel. But he disagreed, claiming Mom would be fine, that her driving would never improve if she didn't just get in the car and do it.

A couple of weeks later, encouraged by Lenny's long-distance prompting, Mom agreed to drive the car, with Dad seated on the passenger side. Not far from the house, she had an accident and totaled the car. Mom and Dad were both okay, but that was the last time Mom tried to drive. No one described to me exactly what the term "totaled" entailed. But I was relieved that, although the car was beyond repair, neither of my parents was hurt. With no car, we needed to hire a helper ASAP.

Enter Sherry Baker.

She was a member of the First Alliance Church. Dad found her through some meetings he still attended there. Those Wednesday evening meetings were the only connection Dad retained with that church—it was the one thing he did on his own. I was mystified by this, as it was so unlike him to attend any event without Mom. It turned out that he had met a fellow there with whom he had struck up a friendship, finding they had many interests in common, and he looked forward to seeing his friend Speedy on Wednesdays.

To find a helper for Mom, Dad consulted Speedy, who happened to be a long-time Lakeland resident. He told Dad about Sherry and her husband, new church members who had moved there from Ohio. They had settled in a mobile home park on the east side of town, and Sherry was looking for part time work doing house cleaning. Speedy made the introductions. Mom and Dad met with Sherry and decided she would work Friday mornings, helping Mom with the heavier cleaning after taking her food shopping. Dad agreed to pay Sherry $35.00 in cash—no need to mention such a small amount to the IRS.

Sherry was a petite, agile woman, then in her early forties. Her work arrangement with my parents continued smoothly for years. As Dad became weaker after another stroke, this help was invaluable. We were grateful for her faithful, steady work. Mom was doing well, still cooked meals every day, and did her best to take care of Dad.

The next summer in Connecticut, on July 2, 1989, my parents were completely surprised to find themselves the guests of honor at the fiftieth-anniversary party I held for them there. Nearly a hundred friends and relatives from New England and New York came to help celebrate at the Pinecrest Country Outing Grounds in Shelton. I knew when Mom and Dad would be visiting up north, so I planned to hold the event there, a few miles from Stratford.

Pinecrest was a beautiful, tree-lined park that included a covered pavilion with picnic benches and bandstand. The weather was perfect as was the catered BBQ. The highlight of the afternoon was the Armenian DJ, who played both Armenian and American music. Most of the guests were not Armenian, and they were blown away by the Armenian tunes and line dances. My cousins and I had formed a kazoo band and practiced a couple of my parents' favorite old songs. Included in our repertoire was Mom's favorite Armenian hymn. I managed to find the music in an old hymnal, which I printed out for our "band," along with the words in transliteration. Our performance was pretty outrageous—we should definitely have taken that show on the road.

Mom and Dad had a great time that summer. Dad's walking was a bit halting—he was supposed to be using a cane at that time. He thought it was pretty funny to stand up, grab his cane, and toss it away. It would be their last trip up north together.

In January 1992, the middle of the school year, my assistant principal called me into his office to take an urgent phone call from Florida. Dad had suffered a major stroke that morning and had been taken to Lakeland Regional Hospital.

I was able to get a flight to Tampa the next day; my brother Lenny was already there. Every day, we took Mom back and forth to the hospital; Dad never regained consciousness.

Lenny selected a bargain undertaker, which I found upsetting, but I was not about to question his judgement. The matter was said and done; Lenny was packed and ready to leave. The next day, the man who arrived at Mom's house from the funeral home was a caricature of the smarmy undertaker, bad haircut and all. I'll never forget his faux bereaved tone when he said to Mom, "I'm sorry we have to meet under these circumstances."

To which Mom ingenuously replied, "Well, it's your job, isn't it?"

I nearly fell over—it was the funniest thing I ever heard Mom say in her life. I just smiled. We took care of the necessary details with him. Mom was a trouper; she handled everything amazingly well. We drove to Tampa Airport and traveled together to Connecticut. Our family had a plot at Lakeview Cemetery in Bridgeport; there my sweet dad was laid to rest.

In February 1992, my seventy-nine-year-old mother began living alone for the first time.

4

WILLADEAN

SOON AFTER DAD'S PASSING, several members of the adult Sunday School classes took on the responsibility of helping my mom. One of her helpers was Phoebe Delamarter. A retired financial advisor, she volunteered her services to elderly people like Mom who needed a hand. Phoebe would go over to Mom's place once a month and take care of paying bills and balancing her checkbook, then send me copies of bank statements along with a letter describing how Mom was doing. She preferred not to make investment decisions, so my husband, Dan, took over keeping track of Mom's assets.

Over the years, the church had adopted an unofficial helpmate system for those who needed support. The tradition had evolved from the principle of caring for one another that was an integral part of Lakeside Baptist.

I had seen how kind they were to those who'd fallen on hard times, such as young mothers whose husbands had skipped out. They were especially protective of their elderly, many of them widows, who found themselves alone and may have had difficulty caring for themselves. A Sunday School class member would stay in touch with the elder person and check to be sure her needs, such as meals and house cleaning, were met. In addition, she would bring her companion to church on Sunday and sit with her during the service.

In 1978, when my parents first started attending Lakeside, one of the couples toward whom they gravitated had been Dr. Hugh Johnson and his wife, Willadean. Even though she was about fifteen years younger than my mom, their energetic personalities were a good match, and they'd hit it off from the start. In 1992, when Mom became a widow and was on her own for the first time, Willadean Johnson was a natural to become her helpmate.

During those years after Dad's passing, Willadean was Mom's attentive companion. She called every day and they talked for hours. She visited Mom and either brought her a snack or they went out to a local restaurant. They often went shopping together and participated in craft classes at the church.

Sunday mornings, Willadean drove to Mom's place to bring her to Sunday School and afterwards to the church service. They were in separate Sunday School classes, since

Willadean was not old enough to be assigned to the "Senior Ladies" class. After the classes ended, the two would meet and sit together in their favorite pew for the 11:00 a.m. church service.

Both Mom and Willadean used to love socializing during the fifteen minutes of down time before the service began. People entered the church's bustling atrium through one of the three glass doors, some coming from Sunday School classes, others directly from home. That fifteen-minute break was Mom's "prime time."

Edie Taylor would unfailingly elbow through to Mom and give her a big hug. "Elise! You look lovely. Did you have a good week?"

"Edie! I'm so happy to see you. I'm doing OK. I didn't see you all week. Why don't you come over after work?"

"How sweet of you to ask. You know, my time is so short between work and getting home to fix dinner."

"Of course, I understand. You must be so tired after working all day."

Then Helen Hughes would pop into the little circle a minute later.

"Well, hi, Elise. Look at you! Don't you look lovely in that color!"

"Oh, thank you Helen. I'm so glad to see you. How is Tom doing?"

"Fine. Fine. He's nearly back to his old self. He's so worried about that mailbox of yours. I know he wants to fix it before it falls down."

"Please tell him not to worry. It hasn't fallen down yet. He needs to get well first."

Those Sunday morning greetings may sound mundane, recalling them years later. But it wasn't simply what Mom said that so charmed her friends, it was more her demeanor. Every word was accompanied by a gesture or smile that expressed her sincerity, her joy in just being with that person. When Mom responded to someone's "hello," it came with at least a squeeze of their hands. Standing barely five feet tall, she would reach right up and squeeze or pat her friend's hand to emphasize how happy she was to see her. There was no artifice in the gesture—Mom was truly delighted to be in the company of every single one. She so enjoyed their chats, she would remember everything—and, when we talked on the phone in the evening, tell me all about the friends she saw and what they were up to.

All the Lakeside congregation loved Mom, though few could have provided the understanding and support as Willadean did. She was an insightful person who understood Mom's needs. She didn't do things for Mom because it was a chore; she did what she saw needed to be done because it made her happy. When they went shopping, she helped her select things. When they went out to eat, she helped her choose from the menu.

Mom often told me about the events they attended together that she most enjoyed, such as craft classes where they learned to make decorative or gift items. Willadean would pick her up and bring her to the classes in the church's education wing. It was a great opportunity for her to get out and socialize with other women.

I had the chance during my visits to talk to some of the women who attended those classes. They mentioned to me that Mom was having some difficulty keeping up with the instructions. But Willadean had a talent for being extraordinarily tactful while helping Mom. She sat with Mom and assisted her, though in such a discreet way that Mom no doubt believed she herself was entirely responsible for completing each project.

I'm sure those classes were Mom's number-one favorite activity. She would call me later the same evening and describe the project she had made in class that day. Her descriptions were so detailed, I had no trouble visualizing her projects.

"*Anoushig [Sweetie]*, I wish you could have been in my class today. We made beautiful little travel cases for jewelry."

"Really? What were they made out of?"

"We made them with some shiny fabric—it feels like silk, but heavier. I don't think it was real silk."

"Hmmm. Maybe polyester?"

"Yes! That's right—that's what they said. Such beautiful prints! You would love the colors I picked: purple and red! I never thought those two would go together, but Willadean held them side by side, and they looked beautiful. She picked the same colors."

"Good! Willadean has very good taste."

"First we cut the pieces into three big circles and stitched the edges. Then we stitched six dividers to make pockets and closed it on top with a drawstring."

"And your jewelry goes in the six pockets."

"Inside the pockets. The pockets are small, so I think it's mostly for earrings and little pieces like that."

"It sounds cute. I'll see it when I'm there in the summer."

"OK. I'm putting it away for you. You'll like it when you travel. That's what it's made for."

"Thanks, Mom—I'm sure it will come in handy."

Since Mom and Dad had rarely dined out, Mom wasn't adept at selecting from a menu. When she and Willadean went to a restaurant, Willadean would explain the layout of the menu and recommend some selections that Mom might like to choose.

"Look here, Elise—these first two pages are all breakfast things, so we can skip over them. If you like, we can get out early next week and come here for breakfast. Would you like to do that?"

"Sure! I never take time to make pancakes at home. They look delicious."

"Good, we'll plan on it. But right now, we need to look at the lunch menu. Look here, this sounds good—Niçoise salad with the soup of the day."

"OK. What's the soup of the day?"

"We need to ask the waitress. Here she comes—do you want to ask her?"

Mom was not shy; she would happily question the waitress about the soup, though not before paying her a compliment—perhaps on her hairstyle—instantly endearing herself to a total stranger.

While they had their lunch, Willadean regaled Mom with stories about herself, about people at church, about what was in the news that day. She would ask her about her relatives up north, and about David, Lenny, and me. Mom could not be happier.

During a visit to Lakeland in 1998, I spent an afternoon together with Willadean and Mom. Mom may have forgotten that Willadean's visit and mine would coincide. No problem, we would all go out together. The doorbell rang at 12:00 noon. Mom and I had been sitting at the kitchen table over coffee, talking about nothing in particular. The moment the bell chimed, Mom's face lit up with the world's brightest smile. "Oh, that must be Willadean! Is it twelve already?" She nearly jumped out of her chair and quick-stepped across the hall to open the front door. "Willadean! Come in. Come in."

I had gotten out of my chair and was standing at the kitchen entrance, where I could see Willadean enter and give Mom a hug. She was slender, with curly, golden blonde hair, and nearly a foot taller than Mom. She had to bend down to wrap her arms around Mom's shoulders. "Good afternoon, Elise. You look wonderful."

Mom reached up and hugged her back for several seconds, reluctant to release her dear friend too quickly. "What a pretty dress!" she said. "Yellow flowers look so nice on you."

"Oh, thank you, sweetheart. I've had this old thing forever."

"Come on in and see who's here. My daughter is visiting for a few days. You remember Mary, don't you?"

Walking arm-in-arm toward me, Willadean exclaimed, "Of *course* I remember Mary. You didn't mention she was coming. You must be so happy. There you are! Hello, Mary. What a nice surprise."

We hugged and sat down to plan our afternoon. There were several restaurants Mom and Willadean both liked; we settled on Reececliff, as it wouldn't be too crowded. We piled into Willadean's car and drove along South Florida Avenue toward Lake Morton. The place wasn't crowded at all, and we readily found seats by a window. The three of us had a leisurely lunch while listening to Willadean describe her many activities during the week. Her husband, Hugh, was a pediatrician, and he had helped her find philanthropic children's organizations where she could work with the disadvantaged.

Willadean had grown up in rural Perryville, Arkansas,

in extreme poverty. Abandoned by their father, the family didn't even have indoor plumbing or electricity. She and her siblings often had no shoes to wear. Since she knew well what it was like to go hungry, she empathized with the poorer families living on the outskirts of Lakeland. A kind, compassionate person, she kept busy helping children who were less fortunate.

After lunch, she invited us to stop by her place before heading home. Hugh had bought her a piano for her birthday and she wanted to show it off. She and Dr. Johnson lived in an upscale part of Lakeland. The homes were larger, surrounded by more expansive yards. Mom had often described Willadean's beautifully decorated home to me. Her impeccable taste was one of the many things about Willadean she admired. We stayed there for half an hour, long enough for me to appreciate the décor and Willadean's own handmade wall hangings.

The new grand piano was perfectly tuned. Willadean's home apparently was not affected by the Florida humidity as Mom's was. Mom's old upright was so out of tune that, the previous year, the tuner had thrown up his hands without even trying.

"Mary, will you play something for us?" asked Willadean.

After all my years of piano lessons, I couldn't play a note unless the sheet music was in front of me. "I'm afraid I'm out of practice. But I think my Mom would like to try it out."

Mom needed no further encouragement. She sat down and promptly played a couple of hymns on the new piano. What a joy for her, and for us to see her so happy. I've always been amazed how Mom could play old songs from memory at a moment's notice. Her performance earned hugs all around; then off we went, back to the car and home.

Once there, Mom insisted we have a cup of tea to go with the delicious Armenian dessert she had made. Called *kadaif*, it was similar to baklava but with shredded phyllo pastry rather than the flat phyllo sheets. Sometimes Mom filled the layers with chopped nuts and cinnamon, and occasionally, as she did that day, with ricotta cheese. Either way, Mom's *kadaif* was drenched in sweet syrup—probably a million calories per slice. Willadean and I agreed it was the most delicious thing in the world.

That afternoon, I had seen first-hand what an ideal friend Willadean was. Mom was fortunate to have her.

A few months later, Willadean signed Mom up to join a bus trip that a group of retirees at church was arranging. I can't recall what historic site they were going to visit, but that wasn't the part that most appealed to Mom. It was the activity itself—traveling by chartered bus, stopping at a restaurant along the way, the songs they'd sing together while riding on the bus. Mom called the next day to tell me about her trip. "Mary, what do you think was written on the restroom door?"

"Hmmm. I guess it wasn't Ladies Room?"

"All right, it was the ladies room, but the sign on the door said *Necessary Room*. Necessary Room!" She burst into peals of laughter, she thought it so funny.

"Hah! What a cute idea. A good name for it."

I laughed along with her. Maybe I wouldn't have found such a sign very memorable, but for her, it was new and unexpected. No doubt she had enjoyed all aspects of the trip; Willadean made it possible for her to go to places and read signs she'd never before seen. I've kept several happy-face photographs of Mom and Willadean together; it's absolutely clear even in a photo that the two were deeply fond of one another.

In 2000, Willadean was not doing well, and Mom couldn't see her as often. We decided it would be a good time to extend Mom's summer vacation up north to include Rhode Island, New Jersey, and Connecticut. While she had been having some memory lapses, I thought she would be all right as long as someone picked her up at the airport.

On July 24, her friend Anita helped her by setting the lighting timers in the house and then escorted her right to the gate at Tampa for a direct flight to Providence. Anita was sure Mom was not aware that she would be away for a full month. Mom stayed in Cranston for a week at her sister Aranoush's apartment. Her husband, John, was not well and demanded a lot of Aranoush's time, so she couldn't fuss over Mom quite as much. After that week, Aranoush's daughter, Rita, put Mom on a plane to Newark.

When I picked her up at the airport, I saw that she had difficulty walking. Her bursitis had apparently flared up, and no one had noticed.

We took a taxi to Hoboken, and I helped Mom unpack. I couldn't believe what she had brought in her suitcase. Besides the blouse and skirt she was wearing, the suitcase contained three slips, six aprons, two sweaters, and one nightgown. Could Aranoush not have noticed how ill-prepared Mom was? Another thing no one in Rhode Island had noticed was that she hadn't bathed the entire week she was there. I made sure she had a bath before we ventured out again.

I took a look at her blouse and skirt and saw they were soiled. The skirt was literally covered with stains. As soon as she went to sleep, I washed them, first by hand and then in the machine. They looked better after that, but not perfect.

We spent most of the week going back and forth to Manhattan. Mom loved taking the ferry, from which the entire New York City skyline could be seen. One of our first purchases was a couple of comfortable dresses for her. One day that week, we stayed home and worked in the garden together. Mom enjoyed working on "projects" like repotting plants.

On Wednesday, August 16, we went to Grand Central

and took the train to Stratford to see Cousin Bob and his family. I think Mom enjoyed that day the most, talking about old times with Bob and his wife Maryanne.

The highlight of our next week in Jersey was on Saturday when we had guests over to spend the day. Dan's parents, Bill and Jean Cox, drove in from Pennsylvania, and our cousins Hamo and Nevart Darmanian came in from Queens. We hadn't all been together for over ten years.

It turned out to be a fun two weeks for Mom, though I'm sure by the end of August she was happy to go back home to Florida. Before leaving, Mom gave me one of the aprons she had brought. It was a pretty little half-apron she had made herself years before.

We exchanged lots of hugs and kisses at the airport. I told Mom the summer wasn't over yet—I'd be seeing her in exactly one week, when I'd be coming to Florida. No, Dan wasn't going to come with me. We had some appointments to keep when I got there—Dr. Young and others.

Willadean's illness was serious—she was diagnosed with Ewing's sarcoma, a form of cancer. Dr. Johnson found the best treatment he could for her. For a while, she'd seem better; then she'd get worse again. Mom worried and prayed for her constantly.

Willadean succumbed to cancer on April 27, 2001, at the age of seventy-two. Her death crushed my mother. She grieved for months, questioning God's reasons for taking Willadean instead of her. Many from Lakeside tried to console Mom, and she was grateful for them, but no one could take Willadean's place. After a few months following her passing, Willadean's husband, Dr. Hugh Johnson, took Mom under his wing as best he could.

Hugh Johnson was a "character"—boisterous, loudly affectionate, always laughing and joking with people. Hugh and Willadean were completely opposite in their manner— he brash, she composed and soft-spoken. They had made a beautiful couple, he with his head of shiny silver hair, both were tall and good-looking. After they married and settled in Lakeland, Hugh had become established as a leading pediatrician in town; both had been instrumental in building the thriving Lakeside Baptist community.

Hugh was fond of Mom and resolved to try and pick up where Willadean had left off. He would call Mom during the week to check on her and remind her that he would be picking her up on Sunday morning. When Sunday came along, Mom had often lost track of time and was not ready to go out. Hugh would wait patiently for her to get dressed, though they would frequently wind up being late. After a few weeks of this, he began calling her as soon as he got up on Sunday morning. He became her alarm clock, so she could get up and be prepared to go out by 9:45.

After church, they would go to Cleveland Heights, the country club where Hugh was a member, and have an elaborate lunch in the dining room. Other church members joined them, so those lunches became a gala affair that

Mom enjoyed. The camaraderie of friends each Sunday afternoon helped take her mind off the looming absence of Willadean.

Starting around that time, Mom's friends gradually became aware that she was not her old self. Her memory issues were noticeable, and she was having difficulty managing on her own. Most upsetting for me was a call from Anita Rucker, one of Mom's best friends. She called to let me know that Mom was having problems remembering things. She thought that perhaps Hugh or someone else had already informed me, but decided to verify that I knew what was happening.

My heart sank. I told her no, that I hadn't heard from anyone. She was a reserved, gentle person and wouldn't have called if the situation hadn't been serious.

She described several "incidents" that were concerning and might demand my attention. First of all, she advised me that someone needed to call pest control. For some time, she had noticed there were signs of infestation in the house. Then she had talked to Charles Hodges, a friend from church, during the week, and he'd confided to her that, when he and his wife had dinner at Mom's place recently, he'd seen a dead rat in the corner of her living room.

Another problem was the late-night phone calls. On some nights, Mom's feeling of loneliness overwhelmed her, and she would call people to ask if they would come over and sleep at her home. Anita named a few women whom she knew had received those calls, calls that sometimes happened after midnight.

Most serious, Anita found, was the food issue. Mom was having difficulty preparing meals, though that did not deter her from inviting people over for dinner. She had always liked to entertain and didn't realize she no longer had the ability to negotiate all the preparatory steps. She had no way to go shopping except on Fridays, when Sherry Baker took her to the supermarket. Anita believed that Mom didn't buy some things she needed on those Fridays, so occasionally there would be old food in the fridge that had gone bad.

I pressed Anita to tell me what had led her to believe this was the case. She admitted, after my urging, that at a meal Mom had prepared recently at which Anita, her husband, and another couple had dined, Mom had served something that was spoiled, and that one of the guests had become sick enough to go to the ER.

"Ugh!" I sucked in an audible breath when I heard that. I said to myself, Oh, Mom, you're worse off than I thought.

I thanked Anita and begged her not to hesitate calling when she noticed Mom having any problems. I had to sit down and collect my thoughts. If diplomatic Anita felt the need to call with that information, it began to dawn on me that Mom must be having a harder time than I had ever imagined. Many incidents could have occurred about which I knew nothing.

So why didn't Sherry, who shopped with Mom every Friday, call and let me know what was happening? Couldn't she check the cabinets and fridge to see what Mom needed? The first thing I had to recognize was that Mom was no longer able to make a complete list on her own of what she needed from the supermarket.

And what about the cleaning? At the very least, Sherry had to be running the vacuum cleaner. Why hadn't she noticed there was a rodent problem? The more I thought about it, the clearer it became that some changes needed to be made.

I felt helpless. It wasn't possible for me to do much in person, as I could only be in Lakeland during school holidays and summers. I was still teaching full time and wouldn't be eligible to retire for at least two years. I could see that Mom either needed a qualified full-time person with her, or she'd have to live elsewhere. We would have to consider having Mom move somewhere where there would be supervision and she would be safe.

I resolved to sit down with my husband, Dan, and talk about Mom's options. Once I was able to think clearly, I'd call my brother Lenny to decide what our next step would be. I dreaded having to deal with him.

5

2000

KNEW I HAD TO CALL LENNY TO TALK about Mom but kept putting it off. I decided to wait until after I took her to see her doctor. I doubted Lenny would accept anything I'd heard about Mom from her friends, "a bunch of senile old ladies," as he'd once labeled them. I had called Dr. Young's office and made an appointment for Mom at the end of August 2000 when I'd planned to be in Lakeland.

That week before my trip was troubling; the more I thought about recent conversations with Anita and a few other of Mom's friends, the more concerned I became. It had become clear to me that I had to be the one to take on full responsibility for my mother's well-being. Dad had always been the head of the family until his passing in 1992. I hadn't been overly concerned about Mom even after that, since she was exhibiting no noticeable symptoms of dementia. Besides, Willadean had stepped in, and Mom had done well under her watchful eye. But after Willadean's passing, Mom's decline had started to become evident.

Mom's friends had come to know me during my visits over the years, and I was thankful they were willing to reach out to me. They saw that she was trying to put on a brave face, but there was no denying that her life had changed. I received bits and pieces of information from a number of them: Betsy Cable, whose entire family—husband and children—were devoted to Mom; Kermis and Jean Frost, who lived down the street on Sylvester Road; Anita and Helen, of course, who would call Mom once or twice during the week to check on her. Everyone at Lakeside Baptist loved my mother and wanted to be of help. However, when I talked to her friends over the phone, their kindness caused them to be circumspect in revealing problems that Mom was having. I often had to read between the lines to understand what they were trying to tell me. I came to realize that there was probably a lot happening about which I was unaware.

It seemed to take forever for the week to go by. On Saturday, August 26, my flight landed at Tampa Airport, where I rented a funny-looking PT Cruiser for the hour's drive to Lakeland. Instead of going straight to Mom's, I thought it would be fun to bring her one of her favorite fast foods, a fish sandwich from Long John Silver. From their parking lot, I called Mom to verify she was home and awake. When she answered, it was obvious that she didn't remember I would be in Lakeland—she asked how I was feeling, just as she would any time I called from home.

She inquired, "How is the weather there?"

"Mom you would not believe what a beautiful day it is—over 80 degrees."

"Really! It's nice here, too. Tell me, what are you doing today?"

"Oh, nothing special. Maybe I'll stop by and visit you. What do you think?"

"Hah-hah-hah! Sure, come on over. I haven't seen you in *so* so long."

"Okay. How about I bring you some lunch? Would you like something from Long John Silver?"

"Sure! I can't even remember the last time I ate there."

"Okay. Well, here I go. See you in a little while."

"Hah, hah! It was good to hear your voice, Anoushig."

Ten minutes later I pulled up in front of 1721 Sylvester and rang the bell; Mom opened the door.

"Mary!" She laughed and cried and hugged me; I wish I'd had a camera.

I carried in the Long John Silver bag: "I'm starving—let's eat."

It was easy to make Mom happy. On that first day of my visit, I figured I'd just hang out and let her talk about whatever she felt like talking about. It turned out that Mrs. Smith, one of the women in her Sunday School class, was weighing on her mind. She had taken ill a few days earlier and been hospitalized. I knew Mom was fond of her—she talked of her frequently—so I suggested we go visit her in the hospital. Wow! Brilliant! Mom so wanted to see her, but it never occurred to her that she could go on her own.

"Mom, why don't I call the hospital to see if she's allowed to have visitors? Maybe we can go there and see her after church tomorrow."

"That's a good idea."

I called and learned that, yes, Mrs. Smith was permitted visitors; I got her room number and the hospital visiting hours. Mom was so grateful to be able to visit her dear friend, but it made me sad to realize that she wouldn't have made that visit had I not been there to drive her over.

I had a list of things to get done while I was in Lakeland, such as taking Mom for a mani-pedi at the nail salon. She got such a kick out of being pampered there but never went unless I was around to bring her. I also wanted to take her shopping for shoes—I knew she hadn't bought a new pair in ages.

The next morning, before taking Mom to the mall, I thought I'd pick up a few things at Publix—just a quick trip for some essentials.

"Mom, I'm going to run over to Publix. Is there anything you need?"

She thought for a minute, then replied, "Light bulbs."

"Okay, I'll be right back. Then we can go over to

Southgate. We'll leave in about an hour."

"All right, I'll get ready."

At that time, Southgate was at a fairly low point. As was true of economic cycles experienced by many other shopping malls, its heyday was past, and some of the stores were vacant, boarded up. At one time, in the '60s, Southgate Shopping Center had been the ultimate modern mall in Lakeland. In fact, it'd been considered such an iconic site, it was used as the setting for the movie *Edward Scissorhands*. Of the sixteen stores that were there when the mall opened in 1957, Mom's shoe store was one of the few remaining. And Southgate's soaring retro arch was still standing tall as a reminder of its past glory.

While I was at Publix, I checked the health products aisle for a pill organizer for Mom. I found a nice big one with days of the week marked over each compartment. Back at the house, I unpacked the bags and asked Mom where to store the light bulbs. She replied that they belonged on a shelf in the garage. I went to the garage through the indoor entrance and had absolutely no trouble finding the correct shelf. Actually, it was two shelves, stacked with at least fifty light bulbs. I shouldn't have laughed, but I couldn't help myself. What Anita had told me was true: Mom was having trouble remembering what she really needed.

We had an appointment at 11:15 a.m. on Tuesday for Mom to see Dr. Young at the Watson Clinic. We were lucky to get a time slot; he had just announced his resignation from the clinic—he would be moving to work at the Veterans Hospital in Tampa. Mom was disappointed when I told her this would be the last time she'd be seeing him.

After a short wait, we were called into the examining area. The instant Mom saw the doctor, she rushed straight to him and embraced him in a big hug.

"Why are you leaving us? I'm going to miss you!"

He grinned broadly; he probably didn't get many big hugs from other patients. "I'm so sorry I won't be seeing you in the future. But, you know, I've had a long stretch here—it's time to move on."

He had me wait outside the examination cubicle. I had a book with me to read and didn't pay attention to the discussion behind the curtain. When the exam was completed and the two of them came back out, he asked Mom to wait a few minutes while he talked to me about her medication. He took me aside and asked who was taking care of her.

I felt goosebumps erupt as I tensed at his question. I said, "We don't have anyone with her—she's living alone."

He hit the roof, at least as much as a soft-spoken Asian doctor could. Their talk during the exam had revealed how much Mom's memory had suffered since her previous visit. He was sure she wasn't taking her medications regularly and was even more convinced that she couldn't be trusted to avoid an accident in the kitchen.

"Ms. Yakoubian, what plans have you made for your

mother's care? You're aware that she could be a danger to herself."

I was taken aback by the severity of his tone. I said, "Well, a couple of years ago we put her name on the waiting list at Florida Presbyterian Homes, but I have no idea when her name might come up for a place there."

"Good, that's an excellent setting for your mother. But the waiting time is over. If you can't get her in there, then you need to look at other options. She should not be living alone."

"Dr. Young, I haven't thought about anyplace else. Presbyterian was highly recommended. And even if my mother is accepted there, she is definitely not going to like the idea of moving anywhere."

"Now, listen—I'm being frank with you. No one likes the idea of moving at first. But even if you have to take her kicking and screaming, you must do it. You need to take care of your mother."

"Wow, Doctor—thank you for being so honest."

Mom and I drove back home; I could barely speak. I'd never expected Dr. Young to be so forceful.

I didn't have much time to think about him, though, since I'd made an appointment for Mom that afternoon at her eye doctor's. On the phone with her the previous week, we had talked about the doctors she saw periodically—dentist, eye doctor, podiatrist—so I could take her to those she needed during the week I'd be there. Since Willadean was critically ill then, Mom had no one to take responsibility for scheduling such appointments. Sherry Baker would sometimes drive Mom to and from her appointments, as long as they fit in her Friday schedule.

We went back home for a quick pit stop, then back on the road for Mom's appointment at 1:30 with Dr. Glotfelty. When we got to the office, the doctor was surprised to see us.

"Why, Mrs. Yakoubian, you're back very soon. Did something go wrong?"

Mom smiled at him but looked confused and didn't answer.

I asked, "Doctor, I thought my mother hadn't seen you for a long time. When was she here last?"

"I believe it was three months ago. We gave her a prescription for new glasses. Now here, these look like her old ones. Perhaps she didn't fill the new prescription."

"Mom, did you get new glasses recently?"

She looked at me, still confused. "No, I didn't."

"Doctor, since we're here, can you please examine her, and I'll take her to get a new pair."

After he gave me Mom's prescription, we drove over to the Lakeland Square Mall to a shop he had recommended. Mom was like a kid in a toy store—she wanted to try on all of them. The shop wasn't busy, no reason to rush; I waited while she tried on several different frames. Her old ones were flimsy and a little bent out of shape, so I thought we'd get a sturdier pair. I picked out four nice ones that would suit her and suggested she try them on. Then the salesperson and I helped her choose one of the four: it was a cute frame, and better quality than her old ones. The price tag was $200.00.

As soon as I could after we got home, while Mom was resting, I called Lenny in San Diego. I first told him about her exam with Dr. Young, and the urgency of his advice. Lenny would have none of it. He refused to consider for a moment that we needed to think seriously about Mom's living situation.

"Doctors always exaggerate," he insisted.

I reminded him that, the previous Christmas, we had decided to increase Sherry's salary so she could see Mom twice a week instead of just once. When I asked Mom about Sherry, she told me that Sherry still came over only once a week, on Fridays. Mom's food supply was clearly a problem; I asked him if he knew why Sherry wasn't at least taking her to the supermarket twice.

"Mom doesn't *want* her twice a week. You can't force her to accept something she says she doesn't need."

It was hopeless; Lenny was always right. I should have said goodbye at that point, but I wanted to end on a less contentious note. So I told him about the appointment at the eye doctor's and her new glasses. He didn't ask why the prescription from three months ago hadn't been filled; he didn't ask what the new ones looked like, or if Mom was happy with them. He asked, "How much did they cost?"

"I recall they were about $200.00."

"What? Are you crazy? What does an old lady need $200.00 glasses for?"

I said good-bye and hung up; I was wasting my time trying to talk to him. Lenny was outraged that I had bought the glasses without first consulting him. I would routinely acquiesce to him, primarily to avoid confrontation. He relished it; I hated it. For the sake of sanity, it was simpler to let him overrule me any time we disagreed. This time it was too late—the glasses had been bought and paid for, and Mom liked them.

That evening after dinner, I told Mom I had a special treat in mind for the following day. I planned for us to drive over to Sam Ash in Tampa. We were going to go piano shopping.

"Piano shopping? But I don't need a piano."

"Sure you do. I have your old one that you gave me last year, and your new one is hard to play."

"What new one? Oh, that black one. No, I don't care for it."

"Wait till you see all the electronic pianos they have. We'll find one that's easier to play."

The next day, we climbed into the PT Cruiser and drove off on I-4 to Tampa.

Here's the piano story. For the previous two or three years, Mom had been urging me repeatedly to take her piano. I'm not sure why, after twenty years, she wanted me to have it. Each time she asked, I rejected the idea; I was perfectly happy with my electronic keyboard, and I could easily buy a piano in New York if I wanted a full-size one. It may have had something to do with the piano's problematic tuning, which I later learned could no longer be easily corrected. Many of the metal components inside the piano had deteriorated as a result of excessive humidity. Whenever anyone played the piano, it was obvious it needed tuning. The piano was a Yamaha upright, bought in 1978 for all of $1,700.00.

I'm sure Mom felt some attachment to it and believed I would value having it. I finally relented and accepted the gift. It cost more to ship it than it was worth. The tuner I contacted in New Jersey told me that repairing it would *definitely* cost more than it was worth. Dan and I went to Frank and Camille's piano store on West Fifty-seventh in Manhattan and bought a Yamaha baby grand. The delivery people generously carted away the upright at no extra charge.

Meanwhile, no sooner did Mom's piano leave her house than she began lamenting its absence. She missed her piano. My idea to make up for its loss was to buy her an electronic keyboard; it was not a great idea. Problem number one was the size: it had only seventy-six keys as opposed to the eighty-eight on a full-sized piano. Problem number two: there were too many buttons and lights, making it complicated to turn on and off. If you just sat down and tried to play it, no sound would come out.

I needed to solve the piano situation. I looked into what was easy to operate, had eighty-eight keys, and also wouldn't be affected by the humidity. The answer was a Clavinova, an electronic piano that had the exact touch and sound of a real instrument.

When Mom and I walked into Sam Ash, we were awestruck by the huge variety on display. It was a cavernous space jam-packed with wall-to-wall instruments. A salesman ushered us into a smaller glass-walled room where the electronic pianos were housed and, indicating the model of Clavinova that I'd considered, he invited Mom to try it out. In one minute flat, with no hesitation whatsoever, she sat down and started playing away on that piano. She played a four-bar intro, then launched into a full-throated rendition of "What A Friend We Have In Jesus." She didn't even need to look at the keys—she looked at us and smiled as she played a second verse. The salesman and I both applauded. With barely a break in between, Mom dove right into a couple of verses of "Blessed Assurance," closing with a flourish at the end all the way up three octaves. I had tears in my eyes. Here was an elderly woman with encroaching dementia, but she could play on that piano as I never could in my wildest imagination. We bought Mom the Clavinova.

I was glad the new piano would be delivered just two

days later, on Friday, while I was still in Lakeland. We'd have enough time to move whatever furniture was necessary in order to set it up in a corner of the living room. I gave Sherry a call to let her know she could have Friday off. I would take care of vacuuming the carpets, which is pretty much all she did after taking Mom to the bank and the supermarket.

Meanwhile, I needed to finish sewing a dress I had started making for Mom. She'd liked the one I wore during my last visit—a blue batik print I'd made for myself. She'd ooh-ed and aah-ed about it, said she wished she could find one like it in her size. I told her I'd make one for her, assuming I could get more of the same fabric. The style was pretty simple—it was an A-line dress with short sleeves and a boat neckline, the type of neckline I preferred as it allowed for wearing a necklace of any length with it.

I had gone back to P & S Fabrics in Manhattan and been able to get three more yards of the same fabric. I cut out the dress and sewed it partly together so I could have it ready for Mom to try on before finishing and hemming it. Our piano shopping out of the way on Wednesday, the next day's agenda included time for completing the dress.

"Mom, before we go anywhere today, let's try on your dress so I can finish it for you."

"Which dress am I going to try on?"

"Here, it's right here. Remember, last time you liked mine and I said I'd make one just like it for you?"

Uh-oh. Too late to realize my mistake: you're supposed to avoid using the word "remember" when talking to people with dementia. I hadn't internalized that rule yet.

"That's a pretty color. You made it for me?"

"Well, I started it at home, but you need to try it on to make sure it fits all right. Then I'll finish the side seams and the hem."

"But the sewing machine is broken. It needs to be fixed."

". . .It's broken? When did that happen? OK, I can take it to the repairman right away. Maybe he can have it ready before I go back home."

"Do you know how to get to the repair place?"

"I can look it up—I'm pretty sure I've been there before. Let me first take a look at the machine—maybe I can figure out what's wrong with it."

The machine looked like it hadn't been used in a while, and some old fabric remnants had been piled on top of it. I threaded the machine with my blue thread, then found the plug and inserted it in the wall socket. To test it, I took out a scrap of fabric and secured it under the presser foot. The machine was operated with a knee pedal. I set the stitch length to number 2 and pressed on the pedal; the machine worked perfectly.

"Look, Mom, I fixed your machine!"

"Really! How did you know how to fix it?"

I laughed, then switched attention to the dress to be finished. "OK, let's try on the dress to see how it looks on you."

We took off Mom's flowered cotton duster and slipped on the blue batik. It was mostly finished, except for the side seams, which I had only basted together.

"That color looks great on you. If I take it in an inch on the sides, it will fit perfectly."

She patted the dress, tugged it here and there: "I don't like this kind of dress."

No problem; with no more comments about remembering, we took the dress off. Sure, I felt bad that Mom didn't like the dress after all, but I felt worse seeing that her memory had declined so sharply.

Next stop: Beall's Outlet for a ready-to-wear dress. Beall's was a lot like TJ Maxx—lots of variety, but everything squished tightly together on the racks. It was the type of store that carried the comfy cotton dusters Mom favored. We spent an hour there and chose seven or eight dresses. I would follow the routine I'd established years earlier after seeing it was too much of a hassle for Mom to try them on in the store's tiny dressing room. I'd just buy all the good choices; she would try them on at home at her leisure and then choose her favorites. My job would be to take all the unwanted dresses back for a refund. The system worked.

When we got back home, we left the new dresses strewn across Mom's bed and freshened up for one more scheduled appointment. We were to see Dr. Abbott, Mom's dentist, in Bartow at 3:30. I had convinced Mom that she needed to be fitted for a new set of dentures. She'd had the same set since the 1970s, and they were discolored and worn.

Dr. Abbott took an impression, and we made a follow-up appointment in three weeks for the first fitting. We decided to schedule the appointment on a Friday, Sherry's usual day, so she could drive Mom over. Since Sherry was being paid an increased rate, I was sure that adding an extra hour to take Mom to Bartow and back wouldn't be a problem.

Friday morning, I took out the vacuum cleaner, since I knew Sherry was off. It was a good thing I did—the carpets were none too clean. I went around to vacuum behind the TV stand and was grossed out. I found there the dried-up carcasses of half a dozen palmetto bugs. I wonder when the last time had been that any cleaning was done.

After I got the bug mess cleaned up, I took out fresh sheets and towels. What I found in the bedroom was just as disgusting. When I took off the pillowcases, I found that the pillows had turned brown, chocolate brown, from years of perspiration. I checked the time—it was still pretty early. I could drive to the mall and back before the Sam Ash delivery. I told Mom I'd be right back, that I needed to run a quick errand. I stuffed the pillows in a trash bag, drove behind the mall stores, and tossed the bag in a dumpster. I ran in and did some really quick pillow shopping. As soon as I returned, I slipped the pillow cases on the new pillows and finished making the bed. I didn't say a word to Mom. I have no idea if she noticed the pillows were any different.

While we waited for the piano delivery, I called Michelle Sasser, a member at Lakeside Baptist whom Pastor Sherouse had recommended. Michelle's husband, Bryan, had helped Mom in the past when she needed odd jobs done around the house. Michelle was an energetic young woman who happened to be a great cook. I knew she didn't have a full-time job—she worked a couple of days in the church kitchen and did child care another two or three days. She agreed to come in and help Mom twice a week, on Monday and Wednesday, starting immediately. Since Mom knew and liked the young couple, she was happy to hear Michelle would be spending time with her on a regular basis.

I showed Mom the pill organizer that I'd filled with her medications; she said she understood how to use it. We decided the best place to keep it was right next to the phone. I planned to talk to Michelle about refilling the container once a week. I wouldn't return to Lakeland till December—having Michelle there would put my mind at rest till then.

After spending a busy week together, taking care of needed errands, Mom seemed to be content. But I wasn't sleeping well after my talk with Dr. Young. He had made it clear that I had some serious decisions to make, and I didn't relish the prospect. As soon as I got back home, I'd be sure to call and check on the status of our application at

Florida Presbyterian Homes.

Dan had been able to arrange a comfortable income for Mom by rebalancing the investments Dad had made over the years. Handling Mom's finances was easy for my husband, given his experience as a financial advisor on Wall Street. He would give me the best advice on what Mom could afford and what might be her most sensible options for the future.

6

CHRISTMAS

LENNY AND DAN AND I HAD, FOR YEARS, spent Christmas together with Mom in Lakeland. It had become a routine that I looked forward to and expected to go there again in 2000 as usual.

Lenny had other ideas. He called me the first week of December to say he wanted us to spend Christmas in Rhode Island, and get Mom a plane ticket to travel there as well.

Why? He had suddenly realized that we didn't see our relatives there enough. They were among our closest relatives, and he thought we should spend more time with them. I told him I'd rather go to Lakeland as we usually did, but I would change my plans and go along with his idea if that's what Mom preferred.

Absolutely, he agreed, we should spend Christmas where Mom preferred, though he was sure she'd rather go to Rhode Island. OK, we'd both talk to Mom to find out what she'd like to do.

Over the next few days, when I talked to Mom, she insisted that she'd rather stay in Florida and have us go there as usual. When Lenny talked to Mom, he would tell me she wanted to go to Rhode Island for Christmas. I was getting tired of the game, so I called Mom's sister in Rhode Island and asked that she talk to Mom herself, with no pressure in either direction. Aranoush complied and called her; Mom said her choice was to stay in Lakeland for Christmas.

Lenny was furious, but he got over it.

Dan and I would sleep in the guest room; Lenny would sleep on the pullout bed in the spare room. The three of us had followed this arrangement since the 1980s.

A day or two before our arrival in Lakeland, a big box from Harry and David, sent by Dan's parents, would be delivered. We'd dive in, picking at the cheese, sausages, and nuts in that box, finishing every last crumb before leaving for home.

It's not like there wouldn't be enough food in the house to snack on. Every year, Mom spent weeks before the holiday preparing our favorites. Up until the mid-'90s, the fridge and counters used to be so full of baklava (phyllo with nuts), *knafa* (shredded pastry with nuts), and *gurabia* (white cookies), and we'd wind up taking some back home with us.

And then the Christmas goodies began decreasing. Each year, we'd notice fewer prepared snacks ready for us. By the late '90s, we'd need to take stock as soon as we arrived, write a list, and make a trip or two to Publix for whatever was needed to prepare meals. The Christmas decorations followed a similar pattern. We were used to walking into a house laden with elaborate displays on every surface. Around the same time as the food supplies started to shrink, the decorations began to dwindle as well. Over the last few years, our festive feelings looking forward to the holiday had turned into feelings of worry about Mom's state of well-being.

On Christmas week 2000, Dan and I arrived to find the front door unlocked. We set our luggage down and I called out, "Anybody home?" Lenny had arrived a day earlier and was in the kitchen with Mom. I was about to say, "Merry Christmas," and get my big hug, when I got a look at Mom's right arm. It was swathed in gauze from wrist to elbow. Lenny was in the process of adding a piece of adhesive tape to the gauze wrap.

I said, "Mom, what *happened?*"

Lenny answered, "It's just a little burn. It happened before I got here. It'll be fine."

I was speechless. It did not look little.

Mom said, "I was heating butter in the frying pan and I had to go to the bathroom. When I came back, it was on fire."

Lenny said, "She had the sense to carry it to the sink and stick it under the faucet—a little splashed on her arm on the way."

"What? Oh, no!" I looked at Lenny's face to see if he was serious. Did he really believe that was a sensible thing to do? I thought everyone knew that's exactly what *not* to do. Rule number one: *Never pour water on a grease fire.*

I said, "Did you see a doctor? Did you have it treated?"

Lenny said, "It's not necessary—we don't need to make a bigger deal out of it."

"But it might get infected. Why don't you take Mom in to have it looked at?"

He answered, "It's taken care of—it'll be fine in a couple of days."

Dan and I went to the guest room to unpack. Dan said, "I didn't see a fire extinguisher anywhere. Maybe we should get one for the kitchen."

"I remember there used to be one in the garage—it disappeared years ago. But I don't think Mom would be able to use one."

"How about a smoke detector? That would go off automatically."

"Of course, yes, there should be one in the kitchen. Let's get one tomorrow."

Dan and I unpacked and started to take a look around. No platters of baked goods had been prepared. The Christmas tree segments and boxes of ornaments were strewn in a corner of the living room. We decided to put the tree together and clean up a little. The tree, by then a few years old, was still in good shape. We'd brought some new ornaments with us, so we hung those on the tree first before adding the older ones.

Mom sat in the recliner and watched us decorate the tree. I showed her one of the new ornaments before hanging it. "Mom, look at this special ornament I found. Can you read what it says?"

It was a large red ball with, in white, the legend *Merry Christmas* in Armenian.

"Oh! Where did you find it?"

"I got it in the gift shop at the Armenian Cathedral. Isn't it cute?"

"Beautiful!"

Dan and I hadn't brought many gifts with us. We thought we'd figure out what she needed and then go shopping at the mall. We sat down with Lenny and talked about what to get her. We decided to pool our ideas on what she needed and who would buy which gifts. Dan and I agreed to get her a set of dishes for every day. She didn't want to use her good china, and she had very few everyday dishes remaining in the kitchen cabinet. Lenny agreed to buy a new blanket, as the one on Mom's bed was threadbare.

The next day, Christmas Eve, fell on a Sunday, and I had planned to take Mom to church. I was making coffee when she walked into the kitchen, still wearing her nightgown.

I asked, "Do you feel up to going to church?"

Mom said, "Maybe we'll stay home today. I'm very tired." Which meant either "My arm hurts" or "I don't want anybody to see my arm."

We decided to go shopping right after breakfast—the stores would be closing early. We first made sure Mom was OK, then went our separate ways to shop. Dan and I found a set of durable Corelle dishes at Walmart and picked up a set of glasses at the same time. We then went to the hardware store for steel wool and white enamel spray paint. Mom's metal outdoor furniture was a mess, badly rusted. A coat of paint would make a world of difference.

I will remember with fondness that Sunday afternoon, the last holiday all four of us would enjoy together. Dan and I went out to the lanai to work on the iron furniture. We had newspapers spread on the ground and spent all afternoon scraping and spray painting the chairs and table. Meanwhile, Lenny was working in the kitchen, busy starting to prepare for Christmas dinner the next day. He had become a skilled cook—we looked forward to a Christmas feast. Mom watched with amusement, mystified by her children's unorthodox role switch.

Christmas Day, the only contribution I made toward our dinner was a vegetable salad. Lenny cooked everything else—turkey, stuffing, eggplant. It was all delicious. The last thing we did that day was to call David on the phone.

He couldn't afford to travel. The four of us took turns wishing him a Merry Christmas.

Tuesday was to be our day of rest. We planned to hang out, eat leftovers, maybe play a Christmas video for Mom. Early in the afternoon, Sherry Baker called, said she'd stop by for a minute to say Merry Christmas. When she came over, she brought with her a plate of homemade cookies. Lenny decided it was appropriate to give her a Christmas bonus. He got out Mom's checkbook and wrote Sherry a check, I think for around $300.00. Sherry looked uncomfortable accepting it. I'm not sure whether she felt it was undeserved or that there would be a paper record of her having received money.

After she left, I started to turn our conversation toward Mom's living situation. I pointed out to Lenny what I thought were glaring shortcomings, such as not enough food in the house. Lenny claimed he hadn't noticed any major problems.

"Len, this can't go on much longer. Mom is not eating properly. I think the only day she has a good meal is on Sunday, when they go out to eat after church."

"C'mon, stop worrying. All old people live on pennies and eat cat food."

"That's not funny. And Mom is not 'all old people.'"

"She can take care of herself. So she had one little accident—it won't happen again."

I didn't want to throw a damper on our Christmas together. I just shook my head an ate another cookie.

The next morning, before saying goodbye and leaving for Tampa Airport, I quietly made a call to Dr. Hugh Johnson and asked him to please drop by and take a look at Mom's arm.

7

PRESBYTERIAN HOMES

RUNNING LATE AS USUAL, I HAD JUST finished packing a suitcase and a carry-on and, at 10:15 a.m., was about to jump in the shower. A cab would be picking me up at noon for the half hour ride to Newark Airport. It was the second Tuesday in September 2001, and I was booked on a 2:00 flight to Tampa. The Hertz desk at Tampa Airport had a compact car reserved for me at 5:00. Factoring in rush-hour traffic, I would get to Lakeland by 6:30.

I took out a fresh bath towel and turned on the bathroom radio to NPR, 93.9 FM. It was not the usual program. The announcer had breaking news: The south tower of the World Trade Center had just collapsed to the ground.

Standing naked, I exclaimed, "What?"

I turned up the volume.

"Wait a minute. No. That can't be right!"

I caught my breath. I think my heart stopped for a second. I envisioned the tower falling over like the tower of Pisa onto Building #7, where my husband worked.

I ran down the stairs and grabbed the phone.

I dialed Dan. Busy.

I dialed again.

Why didn't I turn on the TV? I don't know!

I turned on the kitchen radio. It didn't make sense—it was carrying same crazy news!

I couldn't stop running from the front of the house to the back—running nowhere. Redialing. Running.

Who's at the door?

I grabbed a throw off the sofa and ran to the door.

Dan!

I fell into his arms. He was OK.

Security personnel had kicked him off the thirty-eighth floor of Building #7 before the towers collapsed. He had walked north to the PATH station at Christopher Street and taken the very last train to Hoboken before the system was shut down.

We hugged; I cried; Dan was weirdly calm. He had observed the entire horror show from his office window, which faced the North Tower.

He said, "Why don't you have any clothes on?" We both laughed till we couldn't laugh any more.

We turned on the TV—that's when I saw how the

towers had collapsed.

The next few days were a blur—all flights canceled, all public transportation curtailed. Dan tried but was unable to reach his Citigroup co-worker, Sam Birnbaum. Sam was the one other person besides Dan who had remained on the thirty-eighth floor of Building #7 till the last minute. Sam's son Josh worked for Cantor-Fitzgerald on the 101st floor of Tower #1, and Sam couldn't take his eyes off the flames and smoke that were enveloping the top of the building.

I RE-BOOKED MY TRIP TO FLORIDA—same flight but two and a half weeks later. I also called Florida Presbyterian Homes to change the date of my meeting there with Brigitte Goodmon, their Community Relations Coordinator. Then she wanted to hear all about how Dan was doing after being so close to the Twin Towers on September 11. I took the opportunity to remind her that we had placed Mom's name on the waiting list and made a deposit for an Independent Living apartment three years before and were hoping her name would be coming up soon. She thanked me for being patient and informed me there was a good possibility an apartment would be available shortly. She suggested that Mom and I go there together and we could take a tour of the entire complex.

The day before I left for Florida, I had a phone conversation with my Aunt Arpie (Ara's wife) in Rhode Island. She was a level-headed person who had been repeatedly advising me to find a good retirement home for Mom. She had talked to Lenny as well, and he'd told her that his only objection to Presbyterian was the exorbitant $54,000.00 fee. I assured her of Presbyterian's excellence, and that the fee was well within Mom's means. Her response was, "Forget Lenny. You are taking care of your mother—you must do it by yourself."

My first afternoon in Lakeland, I needed to again explain to Mom the reason why I hadn't come a couple of weeks earlier as planned. Over the phone, I had described everything about the World Trade Center attack and had her turn on the TV to see it on the news. I'd told her about it in detail, and she had been pleased to understand what she was seeing there on the screen. Mom had no trouble following anything I told her, but it wouldn't stick. By the next day, she'd have forgotten much of it.

Since I'd already gone over the story a few times before seeing her, I was able to jog bits of memory so that Mom was satisfied with my explanation. After dinner, I reminded her that we had an appointment to see the doctor the next day; we'd set the alarm to be sure we'd be ready on time.

Friday morning Mom and I were on our way again to Watson Clinic, this time to see Dr. Hix, her new doctor. Lucky for Mom, Dr. Hix was not a stranger—he too was a member of Lakeside Baptist and had known Mom for years. When we got out of the car and were walking toward the clinic, Mom asked if we were going to see Dr.

Young, having forgotten that he was no longer her doctor.

"No, Mom, Dr. Young moved. You're going to see Dr. Hix today."

With a big smile, she replied, "Oh! He's so nice."

I doubt whether many of Dr. Hix's patients hug him when they enter his office. But Mom didn't hesitate to step right up and gave him a great big hug, then began asking about his wife and family. No wonder everybody loved my mother; she herself loved everybody.

Upon completion of her check-up, Dr. Hix and I spoke privately. I questioned him on how pressing our concern should be about Mom's living alone. His response was just as urgent as Dr. Young's had been. He advised that if we could secure an independent living apartment at Florida Presbyterian, this was the optimal time to do it. Getting her accepted at the independent level might be a stretch, but we needed to try as soon as possible. If Mom were to decline further, she would need to go into one of the assisted living apartments, and a change to that level would require a greater period of adjustment.

As soon as we got home, I called Lenny in California. I began by reminding him of Dr. Young's earlier assessment of Mom. Then I brought him up to date, describing Mom's visit with Dr. Hix that day. I did my best to explain the urgency with which he gave me the same advice: we needed to get Mom into a supervised residence like Florida Presbyterian before something serious happened.

Lenny was not interested. "Doctors always exaggerate," he said. "Mom isn't nearly as bad as they claim."

Lenny's response, rejecting a second doctor's advice, made it clear to me that he was in denial about Mom's condition. He thought he was right, and nothing anyone said would change his mind.

I believe that conversation marked a turning point: from then on, he and I would be headed in opposite directions.

I hung up the phone close to tears. If an independent apartment came available soon, we needed to grab it. We would know more the next afternoon, after our meeting with Brigitte.

Meanwhile, I just wanted to sit and relax so I could think clearly. I had to admit, I myself had tried to minimize the seriousness of signs that I should have recognized. A recent instance had come on a Sunday in June when we were late leaving for church because Mom was taking longer to dress herself. I was standing by the front door, waiting for her to pick up her purse so we could go out to the car. She finally appeared, speed-walking toward the door.

"Mom, what happened to your stockings?"

"Oh, don't worry. Nobody will notice."

The stockings Mom was wearing resembled two big spider webs. There was barely any "stocking" left at all—just a few horizontal and vertical strings of nylon stretched over her legs.

"Mom, I just got you six brand new pairs. Why didn't you wear one of them?"

"No, no. These were the only ones in the drawer. Come on now. It's late. Let's talk about it later."

So we went to church with Mom wearing the spider webs. Of course people must have noticed but were too kind to say anything. After we got home, I looked in all of Mom's dresser drawers for those new packages of stockings. They were nowhere to be seen in the bedroom. I started looking around the clothes closet. Hah! On Mom's closet shelf above the dress rack, neatly lined up between her handbags, lay the six unopened packages of stockings.

There was no need to embarrass Mom, so I didn't tell her where I found them. I just took them to the bedroom and slipped them into a drawer next to her slips. I would show her where they were later, after I was able to get rid of the shredded ones.

That wasn't the only incident that should have rung a little alarm bell. Something else had happened that same week in June, shortly after I arrived in Lakeland. I cringe now at the recollection.

I'd been talking to someone on the kitchen phone when I heard Mom rummaging in the refrigerator. A moment later I looked up to see she was munching on something that looked like sliced lunchmeat. I was too late to grab the thing before she had eaten some of it. It was completely spoiled—who knows how old—smelly and moldy. I'm sure I startled her when I grabbed the remainder out of her hand.

"Mom, that's spoiled!"

"Oh, all right! You don't have to get so excited."

I threw the entire mess into the trash; needless to say, I was sorry then for scaring Mom.

I figured, if she was hungry, why not check the fridge for a snack that was edible? I opened the door but found very little—mostly condiments and juice. Then I thought I'd check the drawer on the bottom. She usually didn't put anything in it because the runners were worn and it was hard to open. I tugged till the drawer opened and was surprised to find a Tupperware container inside. When I set the container on the counter and opened it, I found it was half full of *kufta* soup.

"Mom, when did you make this soup? It looks good."

"Oh, where did you find it? I thought it was all finished. Father Nareg brought it—I think it was last week."

"Father Nareg? Who is he?"

"He's the priest of the Orthodox Church in Boca, a friend of Varsig. When he comes to visit her, he comes here after. You would like him. He's a funny man—always full of stories to tell."

"Too bad I wasn't here. So he brought you *kufta* soup all the way from Boca?"

"I'm not really sure where he got the soup. We had a nice long visit and ate soup together. Let's finish it—I think there's enough left."

So I heated up the soup, which I could tell was different from the way Mom used to make it.

But it seemed odd for the priest from Boca Raton to be bringing soup all the way to Mom's in Lakeland. So during the summer, when I was back at home, I called him to talk about his last visit. When I got through, I learned his full name was Father Nareg Berberian. He was pleased to hear from me and forthcoming in expressing his concern about Mom's living situation. He said he liked to stop by and see Mom whenever he happened to be in Lakeland, and that he had begun to be concerned about her after the last few visits. He felt she sometimes was "confused" and often had very little food in the house. When he was over the last time, he'd found a few items in the pantry, but the fridge had been nearly bare. So he had gone to Publix, picked up the ingredients to make *kufta* soup, prepared it, and they had eaten lunch together.

I thanked Father Nareg for his kindness to Mom. I went on to explain that her family had become concerned about her too, and that we were looking into options for the best way to care for her.

The more I thought about the last year or two, the more incidents came to mind that I had dismissed at the time. It took me a while to accept that they had been harbingers of something more serious, not just isolated examples of normal forgetfulness.

It was time that I followed the advice of Mom's doctors. I prayed Brigitte would have good news for us when we went to visit Presbyterian the next day. The biggest hurdle was figuring out how much of a roadblock Lenny was going to be.

Mom and I went out to the lanai to sit and chat for a while. Mom loved that lanai—I could see that she had taken good care of the plants out there, which had grown lush and dense. How was I ever going to convince her that she'd be better off anywhere else but here? How would I feel if I had to suddenly leave the comfortable home where I'd lived for so many years?

Mom sat on the wicker loveseat, and I sat at the little built-in bar across from her. She never sat at the bar because it was high for her and too difficult to climb up onto the bar stools. Judging by the condition of the counter, it was obvious no one had used it for quite some time; the Formica top was coated with a layer of caked-on grime. I didn't mention it to Mom, but Sherry apparently didn't think to wander out here to see what might need cleaning. I had noticed lately a general decline in cleanliness, and began to suspect that she was taking advantage of Mom by cutting corners.

I never considered firing Sherry, though. Besides the fact that I avoid confrontations, I couldn't forget it had been my father, not I, who hired her in the first place. Sherry had been with Mom so many years, I felt it was beneficial to retain her as a familiar presence.

Annoyed about the dirty countertop, I thought I'd keep myself busy by cleaning the bar. I scrounged around under the kitchen sink and found what I needed: scrubbers, cleanser, rubber gloves, and got to work scrubbing away, scraping off the old gunk. I continued to chat with Mom at the same time, but it seemed to bother her that I was working while she was just sitting.

"Anoushig, why are you doing that now? Why don't you come here and sit with me so we can talk?"

I laughed, "I can talk and clean at the same time!"

"But I hardly ever see you. You didn't come here to clean."

"Okay, just give me a minute to rinse it off and put this stuff away. And then I have a surprise."

"What? What surprise?"

"We're going to go and visit Florida Presbyterian Homes. It's that big retirement place on the lake that Phoebe took us to a few years ago."

"You said Phoebe took us there? I miss Phoebe. Which lake did you say?"

"Lake Hunter. Phoebe drove us all around the place just before she moved away. There were some streets there with regular houses and two big mansion-looking buildings right on the lake. She made us promise to put your name on the waiting list—she said some relatives of hers had to wait five years to get in."

"When are we going?"

"We have an appointment tomorrow at 3:30."

Since Mom was stuck in the house most of the time, she was happy to go out for a ride. I wasn't sure if she remembered the time Phoebe took us there, but that was OK. Neither of us had seen the interior, so it would be new to us both. I hoped it would live up to its reputation.

At 3:15, wearing our Sunday best, we drove to 16 Lake Hunter Drive. I made a point of driving around the entire complex, oohing and aahing at the colorful landscaping on the grounds. The majority of the residences were single family houses with attached garages. The larger two- and three-story buildings were occupied by singles or couples without cars.

We parked near the main building and entered the lobby. All smiles, Brigitte came out to meet us. She was a stately woman, around fifty, with wavy blond hair. She said we could start our tour right away and have time at the end to sit and ask questions.

We first took a look at the common room right across from the lobby. It was bright and airy, tastefully furnished, with cozy seating areas on the sides and two larger sofas facing a huge fireplace.

Brigitte then had us take the elevator up one flight to the apartments in the main building. The elevator doors opened to reveal, on one side, a semi-circular, glass-enclosed library and, on the other, a long walkway. The entrance doors to the apartments opened onto this walkway, which extended all the way around the building. We strolled along it, circling the entire second floor. A few residents greeted us as we passed, keen to show off the plants that bloomed on their terraces.

When we had completed the full circle, Brigitte stopped us near apartment #217-B. She took out a bunch of keys and said, "Here's the apartment I told you about." It was right in the center of the second floor, facing Lake Hunter, and diagonally across from the library. The location couldn't have been more perfect. "Would you like to see inside?"

Mom just said, "OK."

I said, "Of course."

"Be careful not to touch the walls. They just finished painting, and they may not be dry."

It was a wide, multi-windowed apartment, nicely designed. All the kitchen and bathroom fixtures looked brand new. The bedroom was similar in size to Mom's at home, though the living room was smaller. However, as Brigitte pointed out, there was a side exit door that led directly to the second floor's common seating area, a glass-enclosed alcove with a grand piano in its center.

The apartment was classified as a one-bedroom, though it did have an added small room that could be used for dining or for guests. I liked the room layout immediately, visualizing Mom turning the small room into her sewing and craft room. She would be safe there, in that charming, manageable apartment, with many friendly people nearby.

When we turned back toward the entrance door, I paused to look through the picture window out at Lake Hunter.

"Mom, come and see. You just look out this window and there's the whole lake right in front of you."

"Yes, it's beautiful."

"Oh! What's that? Look at that white bird standing on the edge of the water."

Brigitte joined us at the window and said, "That's an egret. We have so many of them here. Sometimes we sit on one of the benches down there and feed them. They're so gentle."

"What an amazing, graceful bird! Mom, wouldn't it be nice to wake up in the morning, and the first thing you see from your window is a beautiful egret?"

Mom smiled, "Yes, it's beautiful."

We left the apartment and continued our tour of the two main buildings. Everything we saw was inviting and well maintained—Presbyterian had its reputation for good reason. We returned to the ground floor, where Brigitte showed us into her office.

I had read about Florida Presbyterian Homes, but Mom may not have remembered what I had described to her. Over the past few years, whenever the topic came up, she would quietly acknowledge the need to eventually make some changes, since Dad was no longer around to help her.

Now here we were, push was coming to shove, and I had no trouble reading her body language. Her behavior was communicating that she wasn't ready to accept the idea that the time for change was now.

Brigitte explained the structure of the continuing care community. She emphasized that one should ideally enter on the "independent living" level. When a resident became unable to live on her own, then membership in the community made her eligible for the next level of care, most likely "assisted living." The amenities were available at all levels: meals, activities, transportation to church, shopping. She stressed it was important to understand that, if a resident's health required change, then he or she would continue to be cared for.

Mom nodded and smiled all through Brigitte's explanation. I hoped it was a sign that Mom understood how good the opportunity was. Of course, there was the question of cost. Mom had never handled her own finances, so the figures Brigitte tossed around could not have meant much to her. But since Dan and I had been managing Mom's accounts for the past few years, I knew it was within her means. I saw that I would need to move quickly and set aside $54,000.00 from one of the investment accounts for the life-occupancy fee. The monthly fee was $1,300.00, actually less than her current monthly expenses living at home.

Brigitte liked Mom instantly and clearly was pleased she

would become part of their community. All we had to do was sign on the dotted line. She asked Mom for information: name, address, phone. Mom did fine with her name. When it came to the address, I blanched when she hesitated and then started giving her old address in Stratford, Connecticut.

"1671 Broadbridge—"

I giggled and stopped her, saying, "No, Mom. Brigitte wants your *current* address."

So we got that part sorted out. Finally, Mom needed to sign her name to the application. She fidgeted and hesitated: "Maybe we need to think about it."

I panicked. "I don't think so, Mom. We really need to sign now."

Brigitte and I watched her signed the document.

Brigitte looked at me, smiled, and in her soft German accent said, "Sometimes you just have to take the bull by the horns." I couldn't believe she'd said that. I just smiled back and thought, well, English *is* her second language— maybe she doesn't realize how odd that expression sounds in this situation.

I gave Brigitte a check for $1,100.00 and agreed to hand- deliver our financial statement and medical form within the week. She then looked at her watch and noted it was getting late.

"Elise, you haven't seen our dining room yet. Let's take a walk over, and I hope you can join us for dinner."

The dining room was located in an adjacent building, which we reached through a covered walkway. Inviting cooking odors reached us as soon as we entered. I could see Mom was impressed with the high-ceilinged, sumptuously appointed ante-room. The dining area itself was in two sections: the large inner area was arranged with several round tables; the front-facing area was lined with smaller tables extending the length of the building, alongside windows looking out at a view of Lake Hunter. It was a small lake—we could see lights twinkling in houses along the opposite shoreline.

We strolled around the ante-room, admiring the pieces of wall décor that had been donated by residents. Brigitte then walked us to one of the round tables, where a few people were already seated.

She said, "Good evening, ladies. May I introduce our new resident? Elise will be joining our family very soon."

"Hi, Elise."

"Welcome."

"I'll leave you to introduce yourselves. Enjoy your dinner."

A server brought over menus for everyone. One of the women suggested, "Elise, why don't you try the stuffed chicken breast—I *love* the way they prepare it."

"OK, that's sounds good. Mary, what are you going to have?"

"I'll have the same—and maybe with the zucchini."

During the meal, Mom talked animatedly to the others and discovered that several members of Lakeside Baptist lived there as well. That was great news—Mom would already know some people there on Day One.

After dessert, it was time to say good bye. All the way home, I could barely concentrate on the drive. Everything had gone well; it just felt too good to be true.

8

PENNYSAVER LAWYER

I T HAD BEEN AN EXCITING DAY, visiting Florida Presbyterian Homes and seeing the apartment that would soon
be ready for Mom. It was pretty late when we got
home. As she was in the habit of going to bed around 9:00
p.m., we had an hour or so to unwind and relax. She loved
her tea, so I said OK to having a cup together as a nightcap.
Mom brewed us Constant Comment in her favorite china
tea cups. I knew using the delicate china made her feel like
it was a special occasion.

During the course of our tea, Mom asked a few times if
I was very tired after our busy day. I protested that I wasn't.
We hugged and kissed good night; I promised to go to bed
soon, too.

After washing our tea cups, I got on the phone with
Dan. I was all loose ends, worrying about how I was going

to manage the upcoming move to the apartment at Presbyterian.

I said, "There's still a lot of paperwork that needs to be done. We need to submit a breakdown of Mom's finances. Then we have to get a certified check for $54,000.00 for the entry fee. I hope you can take care of all that."

"I have everything you need in your mother's file. When do you have to give it to them?"

"Brigitte said we should try and get the information to her by next week. There's no urgency, because they're still working on the apartment. She said to bring a swatch or a pillow from the sofa, so they can get the right color carpeting."

"No kidding! That's accommodating of them."

"So the only thing I have to worry about is my cheapskate brother. You know he's going to hit the ceiling when he hears about the fifty-four thousand."

"That's peanuts for what you're getting. The retirement place in Philly, where my parents just moved, has a quarter-million entry fee. . . . And anyway, it's not *his* money."

"I know the fee is reasonable, but don't forget, he still doesn't believe there's anything wrong with Mom. He says I'm jumping the gun. I'm worried he's going to interfere and ruin her chance to get her own independent apartment."

"What can he do? We've been taking care of her accounts. He has nothing to say. MB, your brother thinks he knows how to invest money, but he doesn't."

"Dan, he will never admit he made a mistake. Look, I'm going to start searching around for a lawyer and get some advice. My brother is going to find some way to get his hands on Mom's money. You don't know how devious he is."

"So find a lawyer, if you're that worried. You'd better get somebody local, because the laws are different in every state."

The next morning I woke up before the alarm. I must have had a bad dream about Lenny swooping into Lakeland and using his legal wiles to wreck my plans for Mom. I needed to find an attorney ASAP and figure out what to do. I was so worried and not thinking straight that it didn't occur to me I should have called Anita, or one of Mom's other friends at the church, for recommendations.

Two years earlier, when Phoebe was about to move away to Kentucky, she had advised Dan and me what steps we needed to take with Mom's accounts. Her advice: (a) put everything in joint name, Mom's and mine, to avoid probate, (b) have all bills sent to us in New Jersey, (c) remove Phoebe's name from the power of attorney, (d) get on the waiting list for Florida Presbyterian Homes, (e) have Mom draw up a "living will."

It had taken about six months to make all the changes; everything was up to date.

I got out my calculator and punched in a few numbers. If Mom were living at Presbyterian, her income would remain the same, plus the added income from renting her house. Her expenses would be the monthly maintenance fee, medications, and everyday spending money. I figured she would have a positive cash flow of around $600.00 dollars a month. On the other hand, if she were to remain in the house with the same income, her expenses would include utilities, a full-time caregiver, meals, medications, and spending money, she would then have a net loss of around $5,000.00 a month.

I would never base my decision solely on the cost involved. The more important criteria were Mom's safety and happiness. The Presbyterian Homes offer to let Mom take the apartment on a two-month trial basis seemed to me the wisest course.

She loved to have lunch at Wendy's. I tried taking her to several nicer places nearby, but whenever I asked where she would like to go, the answer was, "Let's go to Wendy's." It was Sunday, and I planned to take Mom out for lunch after church. She liked Cracker Barrel, and we hadn't been there in ages, so I thought we'd go there. When I suggested it, she replied, "Let's go to Wendy's."

At Wendy's we sat in Mom's favorite booth, next to a window facing a colorful bed of flowers just outside. As she did nearly every time, she ordered the same thing: salad, a chicken sandwich, and a vanilla frosty. There was nothing wrong with her appetite! I got myself a fish sandwich and a frosty as well. While we were eating, a couple sat down at a table near us and immediately struck up a conversation. I didn't know them but soon understood they were members of Lakeside Baptist. Mom introduced us and had a great time chatting with them for a good half hour.

It was gratifying to see that she had continued to grow a wider circle of friends. I'd met many of them at church whenever I visited, but running into this couple was evidence that she was still good at developing new friendships.

We finished our lunch and got up to leave, and as we were filing out the door, I noticed a rack of freebie magazines called Pennysavers. I picked one up to look at when we got home.

Mom liked to lean back in her recliner and take a nap after lunch. While she rested, I lounged on the sofa with the Pennysaver magazine. The first thing I found on the back cover was a full-page ad for Mark Dolly, Attorney at Law. The ad included a photo of a youngish, good-looking man with dark hair and a fat moustache, and a description of his specialty areas. Included in the list was eldercare, and across the bottom was his Lakeland address. I thought, *My lawyer search may be over.*

Monday morning I called his office and made an appointment to see him that afternoon. I had just enough time to change into something presentable and let Mom know I was going out for a while. I found Dolly's office on the outskirts of Lakeland, in a single-story square building that housed one other office in addition to his. His secretary buzzed him to let him know I was there. When he came out to greet me, I thought he looked pretty much like the photo, though taller than I expected—over six feet.

My first impression of Mr. Dolly was positive. He was chatty and charming, and he conveyed an aura of competence. I explained my situation to him, that I needed legal advice on how to insure my brother could not step in and jinx the opportunity offered my mother at Florida Presbyterian. Before he offered any suggestions, he explained that if I wanted to retain him, I would need to pay his fee of $5,000.00. I agreed and promised to send him a check in the amount he requested.

Once that was settled, he gave me the following advice: "If you don't want anyone to interfere with your mother's care, then you need to become her guardian." I had no idea what guardianship entailed, but if he believed that was the way to go, then I would follow his advice.

That was the point when I should have stopped and questioned my judgement, hiring a lawyer on such short notice about whom I knew very little. But I didn't. It was a huge mistake.

The next morning, I wired Dolly's $5,000.00 retainer to him, transferred from my savings. I returned to his office in the afternoon to deal with the paperwork. I had written out a detailed list of Mom's assets as of that day. The total, including the house, came to barely $500,000.00.

At this second meeting, he gave me more information about what my filing for guardianship would entail. He explained the first thing I was required to do: we had to inform all members of my family that I had applied to become Mom's guardian. The first person who would receive this notification was my brother Lenny.

The moment I heard that piece of information, I felt a stirring of panic. I could just see him losing his mind when he found out I was, on my own, going to pay $54,000.00 to Presbyterian for their entry fee. Lenny had become so obsessed with counting every penny, he had lost the ability to evaluate any expenditure rationally.

In my opinion, there's a lot of truth to the adage "you get what you pay for." This was demonstrated two years earlier when I had to have Mom's roof replaced because of a series of worsening leaks. The original roof was one of those beautiful terra cotta-tiled versions that used to be commonplace in that part of Florida. But Mom's roof was going on fifty years old, and while we had it repaired several times, the underlying problem could not be remedied without major reconstruction. I went ahead and got bids from three local roofers. The most expensive offer would have involved removing the existing roof and replacing it with completely new terra cotta tiling.

But tile had become scarce, and the cost of importing it had risen steeply. Both the less-expensive roofers would, after removing the old tile, replace it with an ordinary asphalt shingle roof, as had become more common. Of those two, the roofing company with the superior reputation charged about fifty percent more than the lesser-recommended company. When I phoned Lenny to let him know our options, he was not the least bit interested in the reputation or quality of workmanship done by either. Without hesitation, he cast his vote for the cheapest one. Had it been left up to me, I would have chosen the more reputable company, because they would have provided better quality and stood behind their work.

But I didn't feel strongly enough to argue about it, so I contracted the job to the cheaper company. And we got what we paid for. The work was shoddy, and the border area around the garage was drooping. The company had no one available to come over and fix it while I was there. (Today, that roof no longer exists. It had become so decrepit that it had to be replaced again.)

This incident illustrates how Lenny routinely handled such decisions. He never seemed interested in evaluating *long-term* costs but looked only at the initial cash outlay. Knowing this about my brother, I could predict his response upon hearing about the Presbyterian entry fee. It was clear to me that paying it was an investment in Mom's future. She would be guaranteed the best care for the remainder of her life while living in a beautiful community close to her church and her friends.

When Dolly informed me about the disclosure requirement, I tried to tell him what I anticipated Lenny's response would be. I'm sure he thought I was exaggerating. He advised me not to worry, that we would follow the required procedure and my mother's money would be safe.

According to him, I would become Mom's "temporary guardian" until such time as all the requirements were met, such as notification of family members. The grand total of my family members was two: my brother Lenny, a lawyer living in San Diego; and my brother David, a ward of the state of Connecticut, who was never able to recover fully from drug addiction.

On Tuesday, October 2, 2001, Dolly had three documents for me to sign. The first, entitled Petition for Appointment of Guardian, was a two-page form listing eight statements which I was to accept as correct. The statements included (a) verification of my home address, (b) Mom's address, (c) her condition classified as being incapacitated, (c) acknowledgement of the need for a guardian, (d) the value of Mom's property, (e) the names and addresses of Mom's next of kin, (f) acknowledgement that I was qualified to act as her guardian, and (g) a catch-all item stating that there appeared to be no unanswered questions about my eligibility to fulfill the guardian role.

The second document, entitled Petition for Appointment of Emergency Temporary Guardian, repeated the same statements as the first and added that she had been examined by a physician, Dr. Hix, who found that she required twenty-four-hour care.

The third document, entitled Application for Appointment as Guardian, was four pages long; it included thirty questions that I was to answer and sign. In addition to more detailed biographical data, there were questions about my medical history, financial status, educational history, and names of personal references.

I signed all three documents as directed, which Dolly then filed with the Polk County Court. On October 9, the Circuit Judge accepted the documents we filed and issued "Order Appointing Emergency Temporary Guardian" in my name. The order appointing me would expire either in sixty days or when a permanent guardian was appointed, whichever came first.

During this period, while everything was up in the air, I needed to be sure Mom was OK and that the house was kept in order. I had already hired Michelle Sasser to help her out a few days a week with cooking and cleaning. She and Mom were getting along well, so I decided to increase her responsibilities and added a few hours on Saturday to her schedule.

I'd taken off three weeks from work to spend in Lakeland. Michelle's schedule was flexible, so she came over a few times to help me with cleaning. We got a lot done together—Mom's clothes closet badly needed to be aired out. We washed some things, took some to the cleaners, and donated some to the Salvation Army. I doubted Mom would miss them, but I decided to get her one or two new dresses as replacements.

Our nastiest chore was the kitchen. Some of the metal baking tins were so badly corroded they couldn't be salvaged. When we started defrosting the fridge, I got a big surprise. I found a mysterious zip-loc bag hidden way in the back.

"Michelle, take a guess what's in this bag."

"I have no idea. It could be anything."

"It's too cloudy to see and I can't tell by feeling."

I gripped the plastic and pulled. POP! A cloud of white powder exploded in my face—I nearly fell over backwards. Then we both started laughing—it had been some kind of cheese once upon a time—must have been brewing for years.

While Michelle and I were cleaning out the cabinets, I had given Mom her own project. I knew she stored a giant basket full of letters in the spare room. She was a great letter writer. She had stayed in touch with several old Armenian friends for years and kept their letters in that big basket. She had told me numerous times that she planned to go through it and throw out the old ones. So when Michelle and I were working, we made space on the dining room table; Mom sat there and kept busy sorting through those letters. When I peeked in, I could see she was completely absorbed, stopping to open a letter periodically to re-read.

Except for the times when she took a break to walk over to the bedroom. Without our even noticing, she went to the clothes closet and turned off the exhaust fan we had placed in front of the doorway. She unplugged and wrapped the cord neatly around the base and placed the fan in the closet. When we found the fan had been moved, we took it back out, set it in the doorway and turned it on again. An hour or so later, we found it back in the closet. This back and forth happened three or four times that day. Michelle and I giggled about it but agreed not to say anything to Mom. She probably had no recollection of repeatedly moving the fan—she just saw it out of its assigned spot and automatically restored it to its proper place. None of my Alzheimer's literature talked about people doing this sort of thing—it was completely original.

A couple of days before I was scheduled to go back to New Jersey, Mom and I finished dinner early. I thought it would be a good time for me to go over to Beall's and return some things she didn't want. While I was in the store, I browsed around a while before standing in the checkout line. By the time I headed back to the house, I'd been out around an hour. It was dark and a little misty as I cruised down Sylvester Road. When I approached 1721, I saw an apparition in the road: it was the Woman in White. I slowed down and, as I came closer, realized it was my mother. She was in her nightgown, standing in the middle of the street, crying and crying. I think my heart stopped. I pulled over, jumped out of the car, and threw my arm around her.

Sobbing, she asked, "Mary, where *were* you? I didn't know what *happened* to you!"

"Mom, it's OK. I just went to the mall."

"*Ahchigus* [*my daughter*], you *disappeared!*"

"I'm fine, Mom. C'mon, let's go inside."

She probably forgot all about the incident, but I didn't. I lay awake, remembering the specter of my weeping mother in the middle of that dark street.

My flight home was a couple of days later, on October 18. It's a good thing I had enough vacation days accumulated so I could take time off to run back and forth to Florida. Since Michelle would be seeing Mom regularly, I no longer had to worry that she wasn't taking her medications. I had already tried the "long distance meds" experiment: I'd call Mom in the morning to remind her to take her meds, she'd say, "Hold on," and I'd wait while she opened her pill container and took the pills for that day. After a few days, instead of saying, "Hold on," she'd say, "I took them already." That suited me fine, till I talked to Michelle about it, and she discovered that the pill container was still full! Her new task was to give Mom her meds in person.

Two weeks after returning to work, during my lunch break, I received the phone call from the Florida

Department of Children and Families. The caller informed me that someone, name withheld, had reported to them that I had been abusing my mother.

I concluded later that Lenny had probably made that report as a stalling tactic; it cost him nothing. But it took Mr. Dolly many hours of work to interview nine of Mom's friends and prepare affidavits for them to sign.

All the affidavits were similar to the one written and signed by Dr. Hugh Johnson:

IN THE CIRCUIT COURT
OF THE TENTH JUDICIAL CIRCUIT
OF THE STATE OF FLORIDA
IN AND FOR POLK COUNTY

AFFIDAVIT OF HUGH W. JOHNSON, M.D.

BEFORE ME, the undersigned authority, personally appeared HUGH W. JOHNSON, M.D., who after being duly sworn, affirmed, avowed and stated as follows:

My name is Hugh W. Johnson and I reside at 1133 Lake Point Drive, Lakeland, Florida 33813, and my telephone number is (863)xxx-xxxx.

I have been a resident of Lakeland, Florida since 1959 and I have known Elise Yakoubian for approximately 12 years. She and my late wife Willa-

dean were best of friends.

I am making this Affidavit based on my personal knowledge.

I know Elise Yakoubian because we are members of the Lakeside Baptist Church.

As examples of my relationship, we traveled to Israel together once, in 1992, with Elise, we go out together to eat dinner ten or eleven times a year, we attend church together each Sunday, and she visits in our home many times a year.

I call Elise by telephone to check on her. I come over occasionally to visit with her and we just talk about Elise missing my late wife Willadean six (6) months ago.

With respect to their relationship as mother and daughter, my observation is that Mary Beth Yakoubian and her mother Elise Yakoubian have a close and friendly relationship.

I have heard Elise speak of her daughter in Mary Beth's absence, since Mary Beth lives in New Jersey, and says "my Mary [this] and my Mary [that]", and always speaks complimentary of Mary.

My observation is that when Mary Beth Yakoubian comes to Lakeland, they laugh and do fun things together. They cannot do so as much due to the health and mental conditions of Elise Yakoubian.

I have never seen any arguments or strained feelings between them.

Sometimes, particularly since Elise's health and mental conditions have deteriorated, Elise may ask the same question four or five time, or have to be told the same thing four to five times. On these occasions, Mary never raises her voice and never shows any irritation.

Elise Yakoubian has been depressed at times for at least the last two years.

Elise has a three bedroom, two bath home.

Elise's son [Lenny] usually visits her at Christmas, and she usually visits him in the summer, but not this year.

I've seen [Lenny] twice at church, when he visited Florida from his home in California.

Sometimes Elise tells me about [Lenny] needing to be reimbursed for some of his expenses for her.

Elise and my late wife Willadean Johnson were very close and Elise revealed to her that David and Mary did not get along. They still were sibling rivals.

We always spent time with Elise during the Christmas holidays. Mary and Elise always had a good time together in our home and in their home.

Mary calls me frequently about Elise. She has been trying to get Elise in Presbyterian Home for two (2) years.

Last Christmas she was concerned about Elise's mental condition and hoped Elise would be in Presbyterian Homes by this Christmas.

Mary has paid for a lot of things in Elise's home out of her own money and does this with joy.

[Lenny] has called me one time and stated he thought Elise would be able to stay at home rather than at Presbyterian Homes. I referred him to Anita Rucker for up to date information about Elise.

In my opinion Mary would be the better guardian, as she has shown much love and concern for Elise over the years. She sincerely desires Elise to be safe and secure in the Presbyterian Homes.

FURTHER THE AFFIANT SAITH NOT.

Rosalie Richardson, Notary Public, State of Florida

Anita Rucker's affidavit added:

For the last several months, her daughter Mary Beth Yakoubian calls Elise daily to discuss her medications. I have been there when Mary Beth Yakoubian called Elise and walked her through the process of opening her pill container to the correct day, counting the pills, asking her to get a glass of water, and making sure she takes the medications while Mary Beth Yakoubian is on the telephone. These are daily calls.

Reverend Craig Sherouse's affidavit added:

With respect to Elise's relationship to her daughter, Mary Beth, I have only observed a very loving, positive relationship. Mary Beth has phoned me several times to seek advice about how best to care for her mother. I helped connect her with Michelle Sasser, who has been a big help to Elise.

Thomas Hughe's affidavit added:

I have watched the two of them when Mary Beth Yakoubian comes to Lakeland. They go out less now because of the health and mental conditions of Elise Yakoubian. I have never seen any arguments or strained feelings between them.

Helen Hughes affidavit added:

My observation is that when Mary Beth Yakoubian comes to Lakeland, they laugh and do fun things together. Mary Beth takes her clothes shopping. She keeps up with all of Elise's needs. They cannot do so as much due to the health and mental conditions of Elise Yakoubian. Mary Beth comes to care for her mother at least every two months.

Michelle Sasser's affidavit added:

I talk to Mary Beth at least three (3) times a week about how her mom is doing. In September, I saw a burned pot holder in a container of water in the kitchen. I do not believe Elise should cook for herself anymore.

Linda Thomas' affidavit added:

I was aware that Mary was looking for a place for Elise because Elise's health has reached a point where it is dangerous for Elise to live alone. Last year Elise was burned on her hand because she had put butter in a pan and gone to use the restroom. Elise returned to the kitchen to find the butter burning and snatched the pot off the stove to put it in the sink. The hot butter splashed her hand and burned it. This occurred over one year ago, and Elise told me about this about two days afterward. Mary Beth is concerned Elise might burn the house down, forgetting that something is cooking.

Edith Taylor's affidavit added:

> *Mary Beth takes very good care of her mother,*
> *and they have a wonderful relationship. I have seen*
> *that when Mary Beth Yakoubian comes to Lake-*
> *land, they laugh and do fun things together.*

October and November 2001 saw a whirlwind of
activity emanating from Attorney Leonard J. Yakoubian's
San Diego office. Have I said that I'd anticipated he would
go berserk? Actually, I underestimated him. He couldn't
have had much real work to do, as he devoted his energy
to quashing anything I hoped to do for Mom in Lakeland.
On November 9, 2001, his newly hired Lakeland attorney,
Mark Clements, filed a petition to set aside my appointment
as Mom's guardian. (Incidentally, Lenny was able to pay
his legal fees from Mom's estate.)

9

NARCISSISM

NARCISSISM IS A PERSONALITY DISORDER characterized by self-absorption and the need to control and manipulate others. Ranging in severity, some narcissists are merely annoying and thoughtless rather than deliberately hurtful; others are cold and cruel. When the events in this story were unfolding, I knew little about this personality disorder. Since then, I've learned some of the defining traits are:

- A strong need for control
- Low levels of empathy
- Manipulative or exploitative behavior
- Vindictiveness and smear campaigns

Based upon my years of observation, I believe these were exactly the traits that my brother Lenny regularly exhibited. His behavior demonstrated that his primary goal was self-gratification; in other words, he always had to have his way. I should have seen this then, but I didn't.

Psychotherapist Dr. Les Carter, in his online blog, describes 14 types of narcissism and explains that individuals can exhibit combinations of these types. I believe Lenny is a combination of the "Know-It-All Narcissist" and the "Sociopathic Narcissist."

> *Know-It-All Narcissist*: No need for direction from anyone, must always be right, will persuade and coerce, is bossy, gives unsolicited advice, is a poor listener, argumentative, quick to disagree, intellectually competitive, loves to debate with a raised voice.
>
> *Sociopathic Narcissist:* Rebellious, truth is expedient, rules are meant to be broken, no regard for authority, seems intelligent yet also shallow, lies easily, exploitive, user of people, no consistent moral compass.

In my opinion, my brother Lenny succeeded for years in manipulating my mother because of two character traits. One was his entrenched narcissism. The second was my mother's belief, rooted in traditional Armenian culture, that boys are superior to girls. This belief was as confirmed in her as her set of Christian beliefs. Lenny was aware of Mom's trust in him as the "man" of the family and he didn't hesitate to exploit that trust for his purposes.

In some cultures, such as that of older-generation Armenians, greater value is placed in general on boys than on girls. This is an old story. There are still some cultures in whch only men can inherit wealth.

In my extended family, for example, my maternal grandmother, Arousiag, had three children, a boy and two girls, one of the girls my mother. The boy went on to receive an education through the masters level; the girls only finished high school. All three siblings were born in Syria, immigrated to the U.S., and were married and had children here. How have their children fared, boys vs. girls? Arousiag's son (my uncle) had two daughters, so there was no competition between sexes. One of Arousiag's two daughters (my aunt) had a son and a daughter. It's fascinating to observe how she treated those two children. While the boy, now in his 60s, never received an education past high school, my observation was that my aunt nonetheless treated him as the more valued, respected child. And though her daughter went to college and earned a graduate degree, my aunt's higher regard for boys still prevailed. She doted on the loser son, a nice enough guy who couldn't manage to keep his paperwork straight, and sought his advice over that of the more successful daughter.

My grandmother Arousiag's other daughter (my mother) had three children, two boys and me. My brother David suffered with addiction issues for most of his adult life and played only a minor role in this story. My brother Lenny consistently received the benefit of our mother's un-questioning trust, no matter what. In accord with Arme-nian custom, she tended to place greater trust in her boy, which encouraged Lenny to manipulate her for years. Get-ting money from her was only one of the ways in which Lenny exploited her.

My parents' preference for boys was not as starkly ev-ident when we were children as when we became adults. The main reason for this was our age disparity. Had I been closer in age to my two brothers, our parents might have been more open in showing their male favoritism. My brothers were, as I have said, nine and eleven years younger than me, so we lived under the same roof for only their first seven years, after which I graduated from school and moved away.

One glaring difference in how our parents treated us was in our primary schooling. I went through the public school system from K through high school. But our parents gave my brothers the advantage of a private school educa-tion through the eighth grade before transferring them to public high school.

Both my brothers had serious drug problems; our par-ents did everything they could to support them, though mystified by their behavior. I had no such issues, since the teen drug culture didn't exist when I was their age. My par-ents had their sons' best interests at heart, but their permissiveness did my brothers the most harm. David's drug problems were more severe; he was never able to pull himself free. Lenny had a huge advantage: he was arrested at the age of eighteen, and the state offered him, in lieu of incarceration, the option of entering a residential rehab program. That program helped him get off drugs as well as learn self-discipline. But it didn't come to grips with his narcissism. Addicts are known to develop an exceptional ability to manipulate people. Lenny already had years of practice manipulating his parents; his drug-addict experience may have further honed those skills. After being discharged from two years of rehab, he went on to become a lawyer, the perfect profession for a smooth, manipulative talker.

For good reason, our mother considered Lenny her "miracle" son. Everyone in the family was happy with his success in overcoming addiction and attaining a good education. However, those of us closest to Lenny were most prone to being manipulated by him. He certainly talked me into doing things like giving him money on more than one occasion.

After Dad passed away, it became clear that the purpose of Lenny's machinations was to take control of our mother's assets as well as her living conditions. Since my goal was to do what was best for Mom, no matter what the cost, he and I never came to any lasting agreement. He was driven to stop at nothing in order to get his way; I was merely a stumbling block in his path.

What had Lenny done in the past to demonstrate narcissistic traits? For one, he often displayed a lack of caring for other people's feelings. To illustrate, here's a long-ago incident that didn't involve me personally. I recall, during a visit in D.C., being told about an episode that had occurred earlier that week and had infuriated his ex-wife. They lived and worked in Washington, D.C., after marrying, and had only one car. They were driving home together from work with Lenny at the wheel. Halfway there, they approached a strip mall with a music/record shop. A light bulb seemed to go off in Lenny's head—he swerved over abruptly and pulled the car up near the mall entrance.

He said, "I need to get something—it will only take a minute."

She looked at him, sighed, and replied, "Just make it quick."

He took the keys and trotted over to the store. She sat and waited. Thirty minutes later, he came trotting back to the car, plastic bag in hand. A screaming match ensued; she did the screaming, and Lenny did the laughing and fake-apologizing. As I listened to this story, it reminded me of countless times in the past when Lenny engaged in similar selfish behavior to fulfill immediate needs without any concern at all that he inconvenienced others.

On Saturday, February 1, 1992, I had taken a train from New York City to Stratford, Connecticut, on my way to my father's funeral. Lenny had arrived a day earlier and promised to pick me up at the station. The train came on time, but Lenny was forty-five minutes late. The tiny waiting room was not open on Saturday, and it was 26 degrees. My legs exposed in nylon stockings and dress shoes, I paced back and forth, sniffling and shivering, till he finally showed up.

"I've been waiting almost an hour—where were you?"

He grinned, "Oh, no! I thought the trains were always late."

I later caught a cold and had to take the following week off from work.

After five years together, Lenny's patient wife apparently ran out of patience. Taking their young toddler, she left him in D.C. and moved back to her parents' place in San Diego. Lenny was at that time employed in a U.S. government office, working as an attorney. He was sure he'd be able to reconcile with her, so he decided to move to California as well. It was 1993, a year after Dad passed away, Lenny found himself short of cash. His car was in bad shape, and he wanted a new one to drive cross country. He could have bought a car on the installment plan or taken out a bank loan. But in either case, he would have had to pay interest. One of the known indicators of narcissism is rule breaking. Why should Lenny follow the rules and throw away his money on interest? He'd find a way to get around the rules.

Another symptom of narcissism is being manipulative. According to Dr. Carter, a narcissist will have no concern about manipulating even people who are close to him for self-serving gain. Lenny was adept at manipulating our mother. He drafted a promissory note, all legal and proper, in order to "borrow" $10,000 from her, to be repaid with interest. Mom had little idea of the value of money—she had never dealt with even minor household expenses. But accepting Lenny's convincing assurances, she gladly signed her name, allowing him to withdraw $10,000 to buy his car. He never repaid a cent until he was legally ordered to twelve years later.

People with narcissistic traits generally have relationships with those who will easily slot into one or more roles as pseudo-friends. Among these are folks who are fooled into becoming rescuers of the narcissist, people Lenny found easy to exploit. They are persuaded that the narcissist is a victim of others, an abused soul who needs help. These "rescuers" will provide that help without questioning the narcissist's account of his or her behavior, or its underlying motives.

Our relatives in Rhode Island fit this rescue model almost perfectly. Lenny began a campaign against me—went to great lengths to convince them that I was a dishonest person who wanted to "steal my mother's money and put her in a home." They rallied together to provide loyal aid and protection to innocent, powerless Lenny in his quest to resist me. Four cousins went so far as to travel together to Florida and appear in court to testify to Lenny's superior qualifications.

Narcissists will never apologize for what they do, should anyone express legitimate concern about the way they're behaving. Instead, they make excuses or become furious. One popular excuse is that they were only reacting to someone else's wrong behavior that "made them" do it.

Lenny's excuse for insisting on the appointment of an outside professional guardian for Mom followed this pattern. When it proved to be a poor, expensive idea, he blamed it on me. It was all my fault because I, first, had wanted to be Mom's guardian.

Because narcissists don't accept responsibility for things that make people feel bad, when questioned, they commonly take this argument a step further: Since they were only reacting to an injustice, those who perpetrated the injustice *ipso facto* caused everything!

Lenny has repeatedly taken this tack, in one form or another, to excuse behavior aimed at thwarting me from caring for our mother.

For fifteen years I've asked myself, were my efforts wrong? Could things have gone differently? I believe they could indeed have gone differently. The turbulent state of my mother's last years could have been avoided. In the past, my reaction to Lenny's behavior was to chalk it up to his being spoiled as a child. He was the youngest, the baby, and everyone doted on him. I figured all that special attention made him the way he was; he would grow out of it when he got older.

In this, I very much regret I was mistaken.

10

THANKSGIVING

THE "ANONYMOUS" CALL LENNY HAD MADE to the Florida Department of Children and Families was a comparatively minor annoyance; I couldn't see what he hoped to accomplish by concocting that complaint. Mark Dolly had to spend many hours getting in touch with several of Mom's friends and preparing affidavits for each of them to sign. It's a testament to the fondness they all felt for her that they went out of their way to vouch for me.

Right around the same time, in the fall of 2001, Lenny made a trip to Lakeland. He may have wanted to see his new lawyer in person; he also scheduled his own visit to Florida Presbyterian Homes. He took Sherry Baker, Mom's house cleaner, with him on this visit. I believe the reason he chose to bring her was that she was the only person who disagreed with the doctor's assessment of Mom's condition.

He preferred to accept Sherry's opinion rather than that of Dr. Hix, which would remove the need to consider a place like Presbyterian. Sherry had recently upped her fee to $60.00 per week (equivalent to $91.00 in 2021), not bad for vacuuming and taking Mom shopping once a week. Were Mom to move to Presbyterian, Sherry might conclude that her job would be gone. Their visit to Presbyterian was brief; Lenny wasn't impressed.

During his week in Lakeland, Lenny took Mom out for a treat. They went for a walk around Lake Bentley and then went home. I called the house that evening to see how they were doing. Lenny was in a great mood—triumphant, eager to report, "She walked all the way around the lake. There's nothing wrong with her!"

He needed to prove he was right. After returning to California, he requested, through his lawyer, that Mom be evaluated by a qualified person, who would certainly be in agreement with his point of view. In response to his motion, the court assigned Dr. Roy Mercer to go to Mom's home and interview her. I was informed of the date by Mr. Dolly, who also told me the interview was to be private, between Mom and the interviewer, so I was not to be present in the room.

On November 16, I greeted Dr. Mercer at the door and introduced him to Mom. I suggested they sit in the dining alcove in the kitchen for privacy, and I left to wait in the spare room. I was out of earshot for most of the interview, but I did at one point pass near the alcove and heard a couple of questions and responses.

Question: "Who is now the president of the United States?"

Response: Hesitation, "Gerald Ford."

Question: "What is today's date?"

Response: No hesitation, "Friday, November 16, 2001."

Mom's awareness of the correct day and date amazed Dr. Mercer, which he wrote later in his evaluation report. There's a good explanation for this. On the wall, right above where the two of them were sitting, was the "Alzheimer's Clock" I'd bought for her a year earlier. It was a huge wall clock that, in addition to the time, displayed the day and date in extra-large characters. Since Mom had learned to look up to check that clock, she apparently did so without Dr. Mercer being aware. Two hours later, they emerged from the kitchen and, naturally, he had to get a hug from Mom before leaving.

Dr. Mercer's report confirmed exactly what Dr. Hix had diagnosed. He judged Mom "incapacitated" and advised that she needed to either have 24-hour supervision at home or be transferred to a setting with appropriate supervision. Dr. Mercer's fee for this service was $1,678.75.

As the case initiated by the "anonymous" phone call accusation was now closed, Lenny then shifted his efforts to nullifying my guardianship. Following Mr. Dolly's advice,

I had been assuming that, since I was Mom's eldest child, it wouldn't be a problem. In this, my lawyer was outmatched; I doubt he had handled many guardianship questions in the past. He readily capitulated to the proposal by Mark Clements (Lenny's lawyer) to deny guardianship to both Lenny and me. The argument Dolly presented to me was, since we siblings could not agree on who should be responsible for my mother, an outside person, a professional guardian, should be appointed.

I felt instinctively this was a bad idea. When I talked it over with my husband, Dan told me in no uncertain terms, "There goes all your mother's money." He had heard sordid stories about sibling infighting in guardianship cases. The end result with many court-appointed guardians has been the burning through of the elderly parent's money.

I asked Dolly how difficult it would be to retain my status as guardian. He said it would involve a lot of time and expense and, in the end, he couldn't guarantee we would prevail. So I went along and accepted the professional guardian proposal. Once I signed all the necessary papers, the court assigned Dennis Dumont to be Mom's guardian. He was the person in Lakeland that judges preferred to appoint in this role.

Later that week, Dumont called and made an appointment to visit Mom and me at home. When he arrived, I was surprised to see that he was unable to walk on his own—he moved around with the aid of crutches. This didn't hamper his gracious personality—I found him to be a competent, likeable person.

He sat with us and explained to Mom how he would be in charge of seeing she was well cared for. Mom liked him instantly, though I doubt she really understood his role. But she smiled and nodded in agreement to everything.

I had to turn over all Mom's records, including her bank accounts and monthly expenses. I gave Dumont two folders full of paperwork, and then added a third: Mom's acceptance to Florida Presbyterian. We talked about the pending apartment, which would be move-in ready within days.

Most people know enough about Alzheimer's to recognize early symptoms such as difficulty in remembering recent events. I had done further reading on the subject and recognized that Mom was showing symptoms associated with advancing Alzheimer's, such as disorientation. While there exists no cure, I read that patients are helped by providing good nutrition, regular activity, and social engagement. These were exactly what Mom would enjoy were she to join the Presbyterian community.

As Mom's new guardian, Dumont was not about to rush blindly into anything. He said he would take into consideration the views of Mom's children, but where she would live would be his decision. He would need to evaluate her options only after he got the results of her psychological exam. The word of Dr. Hix was not sufficient—he needed to read the report provided by Dr. Mercer, the court-appointed examiner who interviewed Mom. He would then be ready to determine the level of supervision Mom needed.

One of the conditions Dennis Dumont set that Lenny and I were obligated to follow was that we could not both visit Mom at the same time. We would need to clear our visiting schedules with Dumont to be sure the timing was distributed fairly. The resulting pattern had me spending a week or two with Mom, followed by Lenny spending time with her when he chose to make the trip from San Diego. So there was to be no overlap; there would usually be a break between our visits when neither of us was there at Mom's.

I was unhappy about our deteriorating relationship. Lenny and I should have been friends, should have talked honestly about Mom and come to an agreement on what the best way to care for her was. But I gave up when I saw that he had no intention of considering my ideas. I tried to work around him and help her on my own, but he would not let that happen. He had the advantage of legal expertise, which he could use to thwart my efforts and get his own way. He obviously didn't understand that Mom would decline further and her options would become more limited.

In November 2001, I had arrived in Lakeland around the middle of the month and figured I might stay through Thanksgiving, since Lenny was not planning to visit during that time. It was a pleasant visit—I took Mom to see a movie and out to eat a few times. We did some shopping at Publix for ready-to-eat stuff as well. Some of Mom's friends from church dropped by, and she had a good time having tea and chatting with them.

The big project I had planned for us to do together was to write Christmas cards. We went shopping to pick out cards and got four boxes of the ones Mom liked. The previous month I had spent a day organizing her addresses. She had a tiny address book that was completely full, and she'd written the newer names and addresses on dozens of bits of paper and stuck them between the pages. I bought a new book and a Rolodex, and transcribed everything onto both—the book for Mom's handbag, and the Rolodex to go next to the phone.

After we brought the Christmas cards home, I cleared the dining room table, and we sat down and got started. I went through the Rolodex, calling out each name, and she told me whether or not to put it on the card list. I wrote the name and address on an envelope, then gave her a card to write a message inside. The procedure was a little bumpy at first—she got distracted sometimes and forgot who the card was for. Then I found a photo stand and used it to prop up the envelope so she could glance up and be reminded of the name. It was smooth sailing after that. It took all day, but Mom wrote messages in seventy Christmas cards!

On Friday, Sherry Baker showed up as usual. She didn't need to go to the bank or Publix, since I was there, but I assumed she might do some cleaning. She was dressed in a cute outfit, not the sort of thing to wear while doing house-cleaning. She hung around the kitchen with Mom and me until her behavior convinced me that she was on a mission from Lenny. She filled a bucket with soapy water and set it down in front of the pantry. Mom's pantry was tall and shallow, enclosed by a pair of slatted wooden doors. Sherry dunked a sponge in the bucket and proceeded to wipe down each slat on the pantry doors. She continued to talk to me at the same time, asking a variety of benign questions. She wiped those wooden slats over and over, talking non-stop, for over an hour. By the time she quit and went home, I'm sure a layer of paint had been removed from those doors.

The only unpleasantness that took place that week was when Lenny called. He grilled Mom, asking her what we were doing and getting her upset when she couldn't remember things. During one infuriating call I overheard on the extension, he said, "Mary wants to put you in a home. Your house is all paid for—why should you have to move out?" He advised Mom to "hang in there" and he would rescue her from the misery she was experiencing while I was there.

That's when I noticed what was happening to Mom's calendar. I'd gotten her a large calendar desk-pad and placed it on the kitchen counter near the phone. I thought it might be a good gimmick to help her know what day it was. But then each time I looked at it, I saw that pieces all around the edges had been torn off, and I couldn't guess why she had been doing that—until that call with Lenny.

While he talked to her on the phone, she had a pen in her hand and busily scribbled notes on the pad, I guess as a reminder of what was being said. As soon as she hung up, she tore off the edge of the pad and put it in her apron pocket. It was plain that his comments upset her, though I doubt she ever looked at those bits of paper again.

During another call, Lenny asked Mom the name of the movie we had seen; she couldn't remember. She said, "Hold on," while she went to ask me. "What was the name of that movie we went to?"

"The name of the movie was *Harry Potter*." I didn't think it necessary to recite the full title.

"We went to see *Harry Potter*."

This elicited a derisive belly laugh from him; it would never have occurred to him to take Mom to any movie, ever. I recall her having a good time watching the movie, though I was sure she didn't actually follow the plot. She was probably mesmerized by the dazzling special effects.

The conversation slowed down after a few more minutes, both of them running out of things to say. Then Mom, ever resourceful, asked, "Where are you going to go for Thanksgiving?" She was well aware that he lived alone, and she often spoke of feeling sad for him.

Her question must have given him the idea to come to Lakeland. "Do you want me to come there for Thanksgiving?"

"Of course," Mom answered happily. "Of course I want you to come."

"But I can only stay a few days."

"Even for one day. That would be better than staying there all by yourself."

"Okay, I'll let you know when I'm coming after I get my plane ticket."

The conversation soon ended, Lenny repeating the promise to visit for Thanksgiving, though he didn't say when he planned to arrive. I needed this information, since I would need to pack and move out while he was with her.

A day or two later, around the beginning of Thanksgiving week, I began to get fidgety, still not knowing when Lenny might show up. I asked Mom if she still expected him to visit during Thanksgiving, but she couldn't remember. I talked it over with Dolly, and we decided I'd better leave the house by the next day in order to avoid any possible confrontation. I did a quick search and found a cheap motel on the outskirts of town. It was pretty tacky but offered a bargain-basement weekly rate, so I registered for a week.

I called Dennis Dumont to let him know I would be out of Mom's house during Thanksgiving. He had not been informed of Lenny's plans, though he had been given to understand that Lenny would probably be visiting Mom "during the Thanksgiving holiday." I believe Lenny's lawyer had given him that information.

So I packed my suitcase and said goodbye to Mom. She couldn't understand why I was leaving, but I assured her that Lenny would arrive soon and the two of them would be together for Thanksgiving. She asked over and over why couldn't I stay so we could all be together. The best I could do was tell her that Dan was expecting me home to spend Thanksgiving with him.

I dumped my things in the rental car and drove over to the motel on the other side of town. It was bare bones, but it was a bargain and would only be for one week. And it did have an amazing black-and-white TV I could watch when I got tired of reading.

The next day I'd gone out to get a bite to eat and was headed back to the motel around 7:30 p.m. when my cell rang. It was Mr. Dolly. Why was he calling me at this time of day? I pulled over to answer.

His voice sounded urgent: "Where are you?" he asked.

"Why, what's the matter?"

"Are you still in Florida?"

"Yes, I'm here in town. Why are you asking?"

"Can you get over to your mother's home? I think she may need your help."

"Wait—so my brother never showed up?"

"No, and it sounds like he's not going to be coming. I

just got a call from his attorney. He said some health care workers suddenly appeared at your mother's, and she's upset and frightened."

"Health care workers? Why—did something happen to my mom?"

"I believe your mother's guardian sent them to check on her. Your mother didn't know they were coming. Either she was not informed in advance or she didn't understand what the guardian told her. In any case, she's very upset. Could you get over there and calm her down?"

"Yes, yes, of course. I'm about twenty minutes away. I'll let you know what happens."

I got to Mom's around 8:00 p.m. and couldn't find a parking space. There were three cars blocking the driveway. Through the front window of the house, I could see a number of people milling around inside. Another person was standing in the open doorway, about to enter. I pulled over across the street, parked in someone's driveway and hurried into the house. There were people that I recognized in the living room and in the dining room.

"Where's my mother?" I asked the first one I saw, a familiar face I knew as one of Mom's friends from church. She nodded toward the kitchen, where I spotted two women in scrub uniforms moving about. I elbowed my way through into the kitchen and found Mom in tears, sitting at the table. Her friend Helen Hughes was sitting beside her, patting her hand.

"Mary," Mom called. "What's going on? Why are those women here?"

I didn't have an answer, but I gave her a big hug and told her they were leaving—it was all a mistake.

Helen said, "Mary Beth, we're relieved to see you," still gently patting Mom's hand. "Elise called me at home a little while ago. There are these workers here who I guess were sent by somebody, I don't know by whom."

I looked around the kitchen, watching them moving about as if they were in charge. One was waving a pen over some papers attached to a clipboard, the other was at the refrigerator, taking things in or out.

I turned to Helen: "This place is a circus—how did it get so out of hand?"

"Well, I'm the one who called Hugh and Anita; they must have made some calls, too. Elise, did you call anyone besides me tonight?"

Mom looked at Helen and then looked at me, but too upset to say anything. Dennis Dumont's phone number was right there, on a Post-It next to the phone.

"Give me a minute, Helen. I'll call Mom's guardian right now."

"Her guardian?"

I rolled my eyes. "I'll explain later."

Dennis answered the phone right away. I briefly described my mother's reaction to the workers he'd sent.

He said, "We can dismiss them if you wish. But I need

assurance that you're going to be there and will take full responsibility."

"Yes, I'll be here. My brother didn't show up, so I'll be staying here."

"Mary Beth, I visited your mom earlier today. We had a lovely conversation, and I went ahead and described to her the daily procedure we would be following. Whenever one of her children was not present in the house with her, I promised to personally send at least two nurses to look in on her. Mrs. Yakoubian seemed to understand and said she was very glad that someone would be checking on her."

"Thank you, Dennis. She forgot. She just forgot. Her memory comes and goes—on some days it's better than others. I'm sorry your workers came out for nothing."

The women were miffed they had to leave without completing their assigned duties. According to Dennis, their presence was normal operating procedure with elderly clients living alone at home. In his capacity as legal guardian, he employed certified aides whose job was to see a client in the evening, take her vital signs, and write up a report. Also, on the first visit, certain living conditions were to be included in the report, such as whether adequate food was available.

The party was over. Some friends began to leave when they saw Mom was OK. I apologized to those who remained, explaining that she had been frightened as she had been all alone and taken by surprise.

So the bottom line was, Lenny apparently had no plans to visit Mom for Thanksgiving. I suspect he may have looked into the air fares, found they were higher during the holiday period, and therefore chose not to make the trip. The next day I returned to the motel, collected my belongings, and moved back in with Mom for a few more days.

Lenny decided that Dennis Dumont had treated Mom badly, and he was outraged. His conclusion was that Dennis had coldly sent those bossy women to Mom's home without a word of warning. The following week, through his lawyer, he demanded that Dennis Dumont be dismissed as Mom's legal guardian.

II

LONG VACATION

THE POLK COUNTY COURT QUICKLY complied with Lenny's request to remove Dennis Dumont as Mom's guardian. I had moved my stuff back into Mom's when Dennis dropped by two days later. He was gracious when taking his leave, though his post had been short-lived.

I said, "Dennis, Mom loved talking to you—I'm sorry you're leaving."

"I'm sorry too—your mother is a dear, sweet lady. But to be honest, I'd prefer not to work with someone like Clements."

". . .Oh?"

"I'm sorry, I really can't say any more."

"Okay, I understand."

I have no idea how Lenny, in San Diego, had found

Mark Clements, an attorney in Lakeland. From Dennis's tone, I suspected Clements didn't have the best reputation.

At the same time Dennis's tenure as guardian ended, we were offered a golden opportunity to escape the guardian trap. Mom's friend Dr. Johnson stepped up and said he would be willing to act as her guardian. He was someone she knew and trusted, and he would not charge anything for taking on the responsibility. On November 29, he called Frank Rouse, Mom's court-appointed attorney. He described his family's long relationship with Mom, and offered to take on the role of guardian.

He also called my brother. Lenny's reason for flatly rejecting him as Mom's guardian: "Dr. Johnson takes orders from Mary." He said that with a straight face.

When I called Mr. Dolly for an update, he informed me that the court had proposed the appointment of Barbara Keithly as Mom's new guardian. He knew nothing about her except that she was based in Tampa. I learned later that she was a friend of Mark Clements, who had recommended her to the court. Did I have any say in the matter? Dolly knew of no other professional guardians besides Dennis, so he advised that we accept Barbara. He would get more information about her and let me know.

One more thing: Florida Presbyterian Homes had informed him that they could not hold the apartment for Mom any longer. It was gone. I couldn't continue talking to him after hearing that. I sat in the kitchen and stared at nothing. Lenny had succeeded—he had wrecked Mom's best opportunity. And for what? Was it just the money?

The next day, Barbara Keithly and one of her caregiver staff came by to see Mom. She was a tall, pretty brunette in her forties. The woman with her was Sandra Meyer, who would be Mom's caregiver. She was a certified aide, a hefty woman with short-cropped sandy hair, also in her forties. Keithly explained that Meyer would be taking care of Mom six days a week, during the day. She had been given to understand that Mom would be all right at night, provided they took certain precautions. She herself would visit periodically; her assistant, Nancy Bigam, would see Mom at least once a week to see how she was doing and receive updates from Sandra.

Barbara was all business. She seemed to have everything under control. My main concern was that she was based in Tampa, a ninety-minute drive from Lakeland.

Sandra Meyer lasted a full month. Barbara capitulated and fired her in response to Lenny's insistence. He had presented irrefutable arguments against Sandra, and no self-respecting guardian would retain such a terrible care-giver, who frightened Mom so badly.

I was able to piece together the conversation that had taken place between Mom and Lenny after I talked with Mom, and later with Barbara, about what had led to Sandra's dismissal.

I wonder if Lenny realized that, this time, Mom had

out-smarted him—and herself as well. When he questioned her about Sandra, he had asked whether Mom was satisfied with her as a caregiver. Mom could have given any of a number of answers, which included her appreciation of the help Sandra provided daily. She might have described the meals Sandra prepared, all her favorite dishes made with fresh ingredients, and warm homemade biscuits every morning. She might have described how Sandra arranged one of the wicker chairs to fit next to the bathroom sink, just like at the hairdresser. With that arrangement, Mom could sit in the chair with her back to the sink and tilt her head against the rim so Sandra could wash her hair in comfort. Or she might have told Lenny about the crafts Sandra had been teaching her, such as latch hook, and how she enjoyed learning new hobbies.

But Mom chose to describe in greater detail another activity in their routine. Sandra had two horses, a standard sized and a miniature, at her own home west of Lakeland, and a couple of times a week she and Mom climbed into Sandra's car and drove over to see the horses. Mom brought her needlework, so she could sit and keep busy while watching the horses trot around their enclosure. Sandra had sent me a few photos of Mom posing with them. In one she is holding the reins of the miniature; in another she is petting the nose of the larger one. In both, she looks amused by the new experience.

Lenny's response to this disclosure was to interpret

those trips as a negative. When Mom saw that her description was getting a rise out of him, she embellished her narrative. Their talk escalated on both sides, Lenny egging Mom on to provide more gory details of her forced daily trips to the scary horses, and Mom complying according to her own agenda.

What *was* that agenda? I repeat that, as a caregiver, Sandra Meyer was skilled and conscientious in fulfilling her responsibilities. But Mom had never before had a full-time person look after her, and she didn't believe she needed anyone to take care of her. She honestly failed to recognize that she could no longer manage basic tasks such as preparing meals, washing her hair, or doing laundry. She hated the fact that a *stranger* was there all day, every day. The number-one item on Mom's agenda was to eliminate the stranger.

Mom trusted that her devoted son Lenny would take care of it and see that Sandra wouldn't come back any more. It didn't occur to her that, if Sandra were eliminated, someone else would show up in her place—and the someone else might not be the skilled, caring person Sandra was.

The situation, as Lenny described it to Barbara, evolved into a nightmare. According to him, every day Sandra dragged Mom against her will to a faraway farm where she would be in close proximity to huge, frightening horses. Poor Mom was about to have a nervous breakdown as a result of these scary trips. Sandra must be fired!

Sandra was fired; Doris ("Asia") Reid was hired in her place.

I'm not sure how Barbara found Asia. At one time I was told that Asia's husband had done handyman work for Barbara in the Lakeland area, and that she had met Asia through him. Some time later I was told that Asia had worked for Barbara in the past in an assisted living facility near Tampa. I don't know which, if either, of these stories was true.

Asia lived in Lakeland with her husband and three school-age children. Barbara hired her to work the same hours as Sandra had, full time for six days, and no sleeping over. Mom was alone in the house during the night.

When Asia first began taking care of Mom, she was dependable and carried out her duties satisfactorily as far as I could see. She shopped for food and prepared three meals a day, did some cleaning, and helped Mom get dressed.

After Asia was hired, Barbara decided it would be best if neither Lenny nor I stayed over at the house. She asked that, when either of us was visiting, we stay at a local hotel.

When I went to see Mom during Easter of 2002, I stayed at the Four Points Sheraton. I wondered what I would reply if she asked why I wasn't staying over the house, but she apparently didn't even notice and didn't ask.

Mom's friends Tom and Helen Hughes had just recently moved into the Bella Vista retirement home. They had been close to her for years and were delighted we went to visit them. We had lunch together in their dining room, which was pleasant enough, but not exactly top-of-the-line. I could see that Mom enjoyed being in an environment among lots of friendly people. Her comment during lunch: "I wish I could live in a place like this."

Helen said to her, "Well, Elise, you know you can!" I didn't say a word.

The craziest treat I got for Mom was taking her to see *Rent*. A touring company was going to put on the show during Thanksgiving week 2002. I got three tickets and invited Hugh Johnson to go with us. I hadn't yet seen it on Broadway and didn't know much about it other than it was based on the opera, *La Bohème*. We asked Mom afterwards how she liked the show. She said, "It was OK." I'm absolutely positive she understood none of it but at least she had to have enjoyed the music.

My responsibilities at High School for the Humanities in Manhattan kept me busy, and I couldn't take extra time off to see Mom in Florida. I worked as the school's scheduler, a time-consuming position, while still teaching my regular dance classes. In addition, I taught Opera in our Lives in partnership with the Metropolitan Opera, a popular class that required a lot of preparation.

During 2002, I went to see Mom during Spring break, during the summer, and for Thanksgiving. I didn't see her over Christmas 2002, since Lenny got permission from Barbara for Mom to go to Rhode Island for the holidays. It may not have been a great idea for Mom to go up north during the winter. She returned to Florida with a serious cold.

Each year in the past, Dan and I spent Christmas week at Mom's, then went to Dan's parents' in Havertown for New Year. Since Mom was in Rhode Island in 2002, we spent the entire Christmas and New Year break in Pennsylvania.

Dan's parents, Bill and Jean Cox, were a warm, welcoming couple. Jean had every corner festooned with greenery, nutcrackers, miniature villages—you name it. As soon as Dan and I walked in, she urged us to taste the array of goodies she'd made. Our stay there was busy, filled with exchanging gifts, devouring enormous dinners, and shopping trips for after-Christmas bargains.

On Sunday, December 29, while we were there, a phone call came for me. It was Mr. Dolly calling from Lakeland. How did he know the Coxes' phone number? Why was he calling in the middle of a holiday?

He wanted money. Dan and Jean and Bill hovered nearby as he explained to me that he had worked a lot of hours on my case and needed a payment of $10,000.00. I could barely speak. I replied that I didn't have that much in my checking account; we planned to return home the following week, when I could withdraw the money from my savings.

He said, "Next week? That's going to be a problem.

Your account is way overdue. Can you go to a local bank and borrow the money from your family?"

"I don't know—I'll talk to them and see what they suggest."

"Fine. Why don't you do that and get back to me in the morning. I have bills to pay."

I hung up the phone and looked up at my husband, disbelief written on my face. He leaned over to give me a reassuring hug. We'd figure something out.

The next morning, Monday December 30, I called Dolly to inform him that he would receive the $10,000.00 via wire transfer before close of business that day. Dan had looked up the nearest Vanguard branch office and found one in Malvern, 20 miles from Havertown. We had driven to their office, where I withdrew the funds from my retirement account.

We got back to Havertown at noon. Jean had an assortment of snacks ready for us, sure we'd be hungry. Bill and Jean didn't question this "emergency" trip in the middle of our holiday. But Dan and I kept talking about it between ourselves for the rest of the week. I needed to finally realize that Dolly may not have been the best choice of lawyer.

When our holiday came to an end, we drove back to Hoboken on Friday to allow us a couple of days to regroup before going back to work.

The period of calm didn't last long. In February 2003,

I heard from Barbara that Mom had had an accident. While Rolinda Moore, her part-time evening caregiver, was there, Mom had gone outside and fallen. Her arm had broken and needed surgery to set the bone. Barbara would keep me posted.

I called her back a few days later and was relieved to hear Mom was doing well—her arm didn't seem to be bothering her.

Then Barbara called again the following week. Lenny had sent her a lengthy fax saying that it would save a lot of money if Mom were permitted to go to Rhode Island for a few weeks while recuperating.

Barbara was reluctant to allow Mom to go on any more long-distance trips, having seen how she had declined over the past year, and asked my opinion about the proposed trip. I didn't want to sound negative about the idea—I told Barbara how Mom had been doing when I visited her in the Fall. Her short-term memory was virtually non-existent, but she was content in the moment.

The climate in Rhode Island at that time of year was an important consideration. We remembered that Mom had returned to Lakeland from Rhode Island after Christmas with a bad cold. I thought an extended trip might be problematic but said I would be OK with whatever she thought best for Mom. Barbara thanked me and promised to let me know what she decided.

Mom's birthday was in May, when she would turn

ninety. Lenny had latched onto this coming event as an added reason to have her make the trip to Rhode Island, but he needed to get permission from Barbara for Mom to travel out of state. Mom hadn't done all that well the previous time she traveled north by plane. But Lenny had assured Barbara that Mom would be fine, asserting that traveling by plane these days was no more stressful than traveling by car. He advised Barbara that she only needed to see that someone escorted Mom onto the plane, and that the airline personnel were fully capable of keeping an eye on her till they reached their destination. He promised that someone from the family would meet Mom the instant she got off the plane and would not leave her side for a moment.

Lenny further ramped up the urgency of this trip, citing the precarious state of Mom's relatives' health. According to Lenny, they all had "one foot in the grave"—Mom would be devastated if she weren't able to see them one more time. He described how eagerly Mom was looking forward to celebrating her birthday with her family, how it would be cruel to deny her this important trip. Lenny's persistence wore Barbara down till she acquiesced and granted his request.

On March 17, 2003, Barbara's assistant, Nancy Bigam, drove to Lakeland to pick Mom up for the trip to Tampa Airport. She had called Mom earlier to let her know she'd be doing so. When she got to the house, Asia was cleaning up after their lunch. Caring for Mom was taking its toll on her, and she told Nancy that she was looking forward to a few weeks off. She had Mom's suitcase all packed and standing by the door, ready to go.

Nancy greeted Mom: "Hello Elise, how are you today?"

"I'm okay." Mom paused, smiling at her. "Remind me your name again?"

"It's Nancy Bigam. We just talked on the phone this morning."

"Oh, that was you who called?"

"That's right. Are you all ready to go? We have a plane to catch."

"Sure, I'm ready."

Nancy rolled out the suitcase and put it in the trunk, then helped Mom get in the passenger seat. She gave Asia last-minute instructions, and off they went. Mom loved to go for car rides. She was stuck in the house most of the time, so going out in a car was an adventure. As they sped along on I-4, she happily looked out the window, commenting on the beautiful shapes of the clouds that day.

About twenty minutes into the trip, this commentary slowed to a stop. Curious about the silence, Nancy glanced at her and asked, "How are you doing?"

Mom hesitated, then asked, "Where are we going?"

Nancy caught her breath and glanced again to be sure Mom wasn't kidding. But Mom was serious—she had forgotten the reason they were on the road.

It took Nancy a moment to digest that information; then she replied, "We're going to the airport. I'm going to put you on a plane so you can visit your family."

"Oh."

"Are you happy to be going on vacation?"

Pause. "Are we going to visit Anna?"

Nancy was perplexed, sure that no one in Rhode Island was named Anna, then recalled Anna was Mom's sister-in-law in Connecticut, who had died three years earlier. "No, you're going to see your sister in Rhode Island."

"Oh, that's good." Pause. "Aren't you going, too?"

"No, Elise. I have to stay here and work. I promise you'll be fine. We have a seat on the plane reserved for you. And then your family will meet you as soon as you get off the plane."

Pause. "How will they know where to find me?"

Nancy smiled but began to have doubts about the wisdom of Mom traveling alone. She resolved to talk about it with Barbara as soon as possible.

Across the country in San Diego, Lenny must have been worrying about the prospect of losing his inheritance (Mom's money), which had prodded him into inventing a way to stem the cash hemorrhage. Since he had little control over Barbara, he had apparently concluded he would have to eliminate her. No matter that the selection of Barbara had been his own choice, recommended by his own lawyer. She was supposed to "cooperate" with him, but his repeated interference, questioning Barbara's every move, had quickly eroded their relationship, and she had become demonstrably annoyed with him.

Lenny realized that simply switching guardians again was not going to work for him; he had to devise some other tactic. The numerous faxes he wrote made his plans clear: He needed to get Mom away from Florida, the first step in gaining control over her and her money. He found an amenable accomplice in Mom's sister, Aranoush, who, at eighty, was ten years younger than Mom and living in Cranston, Rhode Island. She had recently lost her husband, so she no longer had the responsibility of caring for him. If Lenny could get Mom moved in with Aranoush, he would be able to gain control.

In order to understand Lenny's logic, it's helpful to know a little about Aranoush. She had immigrated to the U.S. along with her brother, Ara, when she was twenty years old. They had moved in among the large Armenian community in Providence, Rhode Island, where their cousins had settled years earlier. Their relatives had helped Ara and Aranoush find jobs, both doing unskilled factory work. Eight years later Aranoush married the man who had been arranged for her, which was still common among some Armenian families.

Aranoush had attended high school in Aleppo, Syria, but was not interested in any further education. She didn't learn to drive and therefore was dependent on others to get around. Here was a guileless, religious person who had lived most of her adult life in the U.S. but failed to learn much about the ways of the world. She clung to the limited role that women were expected to play in Aleppo.

Aranoush was candy when it came to being manipulated by Lenny. All he needed to do was tell her how the "outsiders" who were in charge of Mom's case were only interested in getting her money. So this remarkably ingenuous eighty-year-old woman, living in an inaccessible second-story apartment, agreed to take in and care for Mom. While well-intentioned, Aranoush had neither the understanding nor skills needed to care for someone with advancing dementia.

Once she'd agreed to take care of Mom, Lenny needed next to convince Mom to be re-settled in Rhode Island. That trick might not be quite as easy to pull off as, for twenty-five years, Mom had been living happily in Lakeland, where she had a large, close-knit circle of friends.

On March 17, once Mom was picked up at the airport in Providence and delivered to Aranoush's home, Lenny's blitz began. The strategy was to besiege Mom with all sorts of activities and attend local events so that she would surely prefer to live there rather than return to Florida. Lenny spoke to Aranoush by phone often, as well as to Aranoush's two adult children, planning how they would entertain Mom every day; there would not be a single day spent at home.

With Aranoush's children Rita or Peter doing the driving, their daily activities included visits to local parks and gardens such as Roger Williams State Park. Aranoush made a list of her Armenian friends in the area, and they went together to have lunch or dinner at a different home each day. These mealtime dates were considered the most appealing as they gave Mom the opportunity to speak Armenian with the hosts. They were of the same generation, and most were originally from Aleppo as well.

So for six weeks, Aranoush's family and friends provided Mom with a whirlwind of activity. They were certain Mom would be so overwhelmed she would never want to leave.

It didn't work.

Before the initially approved six-week vacation had come to an end, Lenny was ready to extend Mom's stay. When he contacted Barbara to request an extension, he first brought up the "inexcusable" mishap that had occurred on the plane back in March. He was incensed at Nancy's carelessness when she put Mom on the plane. She had not adequately secured Mom's glasses, and they had been lost, along with her carry-on bag. Her relatives in Rhode Island had to take her to be examined and buy her a new pair. He certainly expected to be reimbursed for that unnecessary expense. There were other expenses as well that required reimbursement: Mom's living expenses, her airfare, and the doctor's visit.

After much cajoling, he claiming that Mom so wanted to stay a little longer, Barbara authorized four additional weeks. When that extension was about to expire, Lenny again assaulted Barbara with a barrage of plausible reasons why Mom needed to stay for four more weeks. The new priest at the Armenian Church in Providence was to be ordained the next week. This was the experience of a lifetime that Mom wanted badly to witness. Rita, Aranoush's daughter, was in the process of organizing a "family reunion" the following week. Mom would be horribly disappointed if she were to miss that exciting family event. Lenny neglected to mention to Barbara that Mom had no awareness of *any* of these proposed events. Mom did, however, frequently question Aranoush about when she was going to go home to Florida.

Barbara approved another four weeks in Rhode Island, but that was the limit. When Lenny began begging her for another extension, she refused to be pushed further. She knew that I had planned a ninetieth birthday party for her in Lakeland in July, and had promised that Mom would be back home well in advance of the date.

On May 12, Barbara finally found it necessary to have her lawyer request a court order be issued demanding that Mom be returned to her home in Lakeland.

On Sunday, June 29, Mom was back at Lakeside Baptist, following an absence of fourteen weeks. The Senior Women's Sunday School class greeted her with hugs all around, happy to see her again. When they asked why she had been away in Rhode Island for so long, she replied, "I really don't know. There was no reason for it. I'll never go away again."

12

ASIA

WHILE MOM AND I SPOKE OFTEN on the phone, it wasn't until July 2003 that I saw her again, when we had her ninetieth birthday bash. The actual date of her birthday was May 30, but our Rhode Island relatives had kept her there from March 17 to June 23.

With Michelle Sasser's long-distance help, I planned the party to be held on July 17 in the church hall. The event was a huge success—close to a hundred friends from Lakeside Baptist attended. Dee Grandbois, the church chef, had prepared two long tables full of home-made goodies. We had ordered a sheet cake decorated with sugary blue-and-white flowers and the inscription *Happy 90th Birthday, We Love You.* We took photos of everyone at the event, Bryan Sasser acting as photographer.

The next few days were anticlimactic, nibbling on left-overs we'd brought home from the party. Mom and I would sit down and talk about some of the people who had attended. I'd take out the guest book and remind her who'd been there, reading each name. When I came across one she knew especially well, she'd launch into a story about that person's family and about some memories they had together.

One day that week, I decided to play an Armenian CD I'd brought as a birthday gift. The music is mesmerizing—sounds a lot like belly dance music—and I couldn't resist getting up and dancing around the living room. Well, Mom started laughing like I've never seen her laugh in my life. She laughed harder, and I kept dancing—it was hysterical. Pretty soon Asia wandered in from her hiding place, curious to see what was going on. She took one look at us and started laughing herself. Bryan should have been there to record that scene—it was priceless.

For the Christmas / New Year holidays of 2003, Dan and I spent the first half of our break with Mom in Lakeland and the second half with Dan's parents in Havertown. When we got to Lakeland, we checked into the Sheraton and then drove over to Mom's place. I had called the house to let Asia know we'd be coming over and not to bother about dinner that day—we would get take-out from Long John Silver, which I knew Mom liked. Even though I'd called to remind her, Mom was completely surprised and delighted to see us. "Mary! When did you get here? I didn't know you were coming! Come here, let me see you. What did you do to your hair? You look different!"

"Merry Christmas, Mom! How are you feeling?"

We hugged and hugged as if we hadn't seen one another for years. Dan stood there grinning till Mom finally acknowledged his presence.

"Dan! You're here, too? Come here, let me give you a hug."

"Hi, Mrs. Yakoubian. You're looking well."

We went on hugging and kissing for several minutes. When we finally settled down, I asked her about her Christmas decorations. There were just a few holiday items on display, not the usual over-the-top decorations of past years. I was tickled to see a favorite knickknack displayed on the sofa table. It consisted of four ceramic candle holders, each shaped like a letter of the alphabet. Lined up, the four spelled N-O-E-L. I couldn't resist going over to the table and changing the order so they read L-E-O-N. It was a silly thing we had done for dozens of years with those candle holders. Asia started laughing, though I don't believe she was aware that my Dad's name was Leon.

I asked, "Mom, do you still have your Christmas tree from last year?"

"I'm sure it's there. It must be in the garage. I need to put it up."

"Don't worry about it. Dan and I will set it up. It will

give us something to do."

"Mary! You just got here, and you're starting to work already. Come and sit down. Let me look at you."

"All right. Let me just check the garage to see if the tree and stuff are still there."

We found the garage was more chaotic than usual and looked as if everything had been gone through. We hunted everywhere, but the only Christmassy thing we could find was one large box of tree ornaments.

"It looks like a lot of stuff was thrown out," I said. "No sign of the tree."

"No, there's nothing here except for that one box. If the tree were here, it would have turned up by now."

"Okay, we have to get one. Let's just go to the mall and pick up a small tree at the hardware store."

Dan was never eager to go shopping, but he agreed that Mom would be pleased if we had a nice tree set up for her. We decided not to tell her hers was missing, only that some ornaments were broken and that we would drive over to Frank's Hardware to pick up replacements.

We sat in the living room for a while and chatted with her; Asia stayed in the kitchen. We decided it would be a good idea to shop for the tree and then pick up some take-out food right afterwards. It turned out to be a productive shopping trip. At the mall we found a cute little pre-lit tree on sale, which we brought home and had time to set up after we had our Long John Silver dinner.

Mom was happy with the tree. Every day that week we spent with her, she ooh-ed and ahh-ed all over again about the decorations.

Mom's gift was delivered on Tuesday, two days before Christmas. I'd bought a large screen TV and DVD player from Circuit City, over the phone, a month earlier. Mom rarely watched TV, but she loved videos. She could watch *Fantasia* repeatedly, as well as Lawrence Welk re-runs. Dan set up both units in the living room, and we spent an evening admiring the excellent reception.

Asia had moved some things around, such as the sheets and towels, which we found were in a different closet. We didn't ask her about it until the doily incident. In the dining room sideboard, Mom had stored two drawers full of antique needlework. There were a number of delicate needle-lace doilies, and several pieces of hand-embroidered linens, that had been brought over years ago from Syria. I opened one of the drawers just to have a look and discovered it was empty. When I asked Asia about it, she said that Nancy Bigam, Barbara's assistant, had told her to throw them out because they were "rotten" as a result of the dampness. I was stunned. It didn't make sense, but I thought to give Nancy a call and ask her about them.

The other odd behavior on Asia's part happened the day before we left for home. Dan and I were browsing through the bookshelves in the spare bedroom, which served as a combination sewing room and office and also had a pullout sofa-bed. The book collection had been left pretty much the same as it had been when my Dad was living. His old hardcover books were still there: *You Can't Go Home Again,* by Thomas Wolfe; *Inside Music,* by Karl Haas; an ancient Webster dictionary.

While we were perusing the shelves, Asia came into the room. She held out a hand, palm up, showing us what Mom kept in her jewelry box: Mom's gold jewelry from Syria. We had known for years that she kept all those pieces, at least two dozen 24-carat gold items, in an unlocked box on her dresser. We got the impression from Asia that she believed she was showing us something we didn't know about.

I looked at the handful of gold and said, "Yes, Mom brought those things from the old country. It's better quality than the gold you find here."

I assumed Asia replaced the gold jewelry where it was kept. It didn't occur to me that it might be a temptation for her. I was still teaching in New York during the first year of Asia's employment, so I was only able to observe her when I visited Mom periodically. I retired in 2003 and was free thereafter to go to Lakeland more frequently during Asia's second year with Mom.

In the beginning, I never noticed her trying to cut corners on the job. But after several months, this began to change. She started becoming careless about her duties, offering excuses if questioned. Nancy drove over each week to check on Mom and reported to Barbara that Asia seemed to be slacking off, taking advantage of being on her own most of the time without supervision. Questions came up about inadequate food in the house, and a decline in cleanliness. On two occasions when she dropped by, Nancy had found that Asia was not there and Mom was seated alone, asleep in the recliner, with the TV on full blast. The first time, Asia had said there had been some sort of emergency at her home. The second time this happened, she'd become hostile with Nancy, asserting that she took orders not from her but only from Barbara.

Barbara was not happy with Asia's attitude, so she made a surprise trip to Lakeland and read her the riot act. With her job on the line, she expected Asia to try and do everything that was required of her. Not long afterwards, I went to visit Mom for a few days; I stayed at the Sheraton. Each time I went to the house, I noticed the conditions there were not up to par as they used to be. The TV soap operas were on constantly, at full volume, while Mom would be sitting in the recliner staring blankly at something in which she surely had no interest.

I saw that Mom no longer was wearing the regular clothes that she was accustomed to—flowery, loose-fitting dusters—but was dressed in cotton elastic-waist pants that Asia had gotten for her. Mom had never before worn pants. I didn't say anything about the change in Mom's clothing, but I figured it was probably easier for Asia to dress her in pants than get her into panty hose and a dress.

On Sunday, when I went to pick Mom up for church, she was suitably dressed in one of her Sunday dresses, but her hair was soaking wet. I learned later that this was Asia's way of combing Mom's hair. She didn't wash her hair, but dipped a comb in water and ran it through, giving it the appearance of having just been washed. Mom was so happy seeing I was there to take her to church, her clothes and hair were probably the last thing on her mind.

What I observed the next day I felt absolutely had to be reported to Barbara. I went to Mom's around lunchtime and saw what Asia had been preparing for her. As I walked into the kitchen, she had just finished arranging Mom's plate of food: a stack of potato chips on one side, and Dinty Moore Stew, still in the can, in the middle of the plate. I was appalled. I believe Dinty Moore Stew is the cheapest, barely edible meat product in existence—it's right up there with Spam. I didn't say a word, as it wasn't my place to question Asia—I'd have to wait till I could speak to Barbara.

I was seriously upset about that food; I couldn't get the picture out of my mind. I had to go back home to New Jersey that evening, so I called Barbara the next day to let her know about the quality of that lunch. She promised to go there later in the week and explain to Asia, in person, what was required of her.

Starting in 2004, Asia had begun to enlist the aid of her

children to help with some of her duties caring for Mom. Her son Marcus, a high school student, was with Asia frequently, staying at the house while Asia ran errands. Barbara had spoken with Marcus and, as she found him mature enough to handle some responsibility, gave Asia permission to have him with her when needed.

At the same time, Mom began having some unexplained episodes that caused me, and Barbara, to worry. Randy, Mom's neighbor across the street, called to report to me that Mom had been seen wandering outside after dark. I called Barbara to tell her about the midnight stroll, and she immediately made an appointment for Nancy to bring Mom to see Dr. Hix.

He advised that Mom must no longer be left alone— someone needed to be with her at all times. Asia couldn't commit to daily round-the-clock care, but said that she could alternate with Marcus, sleeping in the guest bedroom or on the spare-room sofa. This arrangement worked, at least for a few weeks. . . until Mom's vacation in California.

There shouldn't have been anyone in Mom's house while she was visiting Lenny. During the time she was away, I received a call from her neighbor Randy. Marcus was having a party. It was a big, loud party of high school kids overflowing Mom's house. Numerous cars were parked randomly in front of neighborhood homes.

I reported this immediately to Barbara, who sent Nancy to Lakeland the next day. She visited the neighbors to learn the details before informing Asia that she was to be terminated. Asia begged for her job. She cried and apologized. She promised that Marcus would never set foot in the house again. Nancy said they would give her one more chance. The following week, Asia knocked on every door in the vicinity of Mom's house and offered handwritten notes of apology to each neighbor.

Mom returned home from her California vacation in July. Barbara and Nancy kept a closer eye on Asia for the next several weeks and were satisfied she had shaped up.

In August 2004, I got a message from Barbara informing me that Asia had just been fired.

It was another, more dangerous incident that was the last straw. According to Barbara, she had received an emergency phone call from Asia regarding the lights in the house. Something had gone wrong with the electricity in one area, possibly a result of hurricane damage, and Asia was unable to turn on any lights in two of the rooms. She explained to Barbara that she had brought candles over and was using them until the lighting was fixed.

Barbara hit the ceiling. "Absolutely not!" she had warned Asia. "Get rid of every single candle, and do not light one again under any circumstances." She had been terrified; it would have been a disaster if a candle started a fire. She informed Asia that she would get an electrician to go over and take care of the problem. In the meantime, Asia was to stay out of the unlit rooms. If for some reason she had to use that part of the house, she would have to use a flashlight.

Barbara asked Nancy to make a special trip to Mom's house the next day to see what the problem was concerning the electricity. Nancy would be able to readily see if it was just a matter of a blown fuse.

Nancy reached the house at dusk. When she opened the door, she could hear Asia's voice from a distance, talking on her cell phone. Nancy walked in to find several candles burning in two of the rooms. That was it. Asia was told to leave on the spot; Nancy stayed overnight with Mom.

13

TRAVELING COMPANIONS

MY NEW LAWYER, SCOTT LANGSTON, was a proverbial breath of fresh air. I found him through the recommendation of a few people at Lakeside Baptist, where he was a member. He had known both my parents since the '80s. I hired him in February 2002, the same day I fired Mark Dolly. Dolly didn't go quietly. A week later, he sent me a heavily padded bill, replete with inflated and what appeared to be fabricated charges, in the amount of $12,075.00.

Seven weeks after Mom's return from her long vacation, Lenny filed for a guardianship hearing to be held at the Polk County Courthouse in Bartow, Florida. Judge Ronald Herring was assigned the case, and the hearing was scheduled for October 27 and 28, 2003. The time reserved for the hearing was one and one-half days. My brother Lenny had two objectives in requesting this hearing. The first was to permit him to move Mom permanently to Rhode Island, where she would live with, and be cared for, by her eighty-year-old sister, Aranoush. The second was to remove Barbara Keithly as Mom's legal guardian and replace her with a co-guardianship, which would consist of Mom's brother, Ara, Mom's niece Rita (daughter of Aranoush), and Lenny himself.

I was concerned about Lenny's idea to relocate Mom to Rhode Island for several reasons. The colder climate, the inaccessible second-floor apartment, Aranoush's limitations, and the loss of friends and church community were all serious drawbacks. I couldn't think of a logical reason for uprooting my mother, except for one: money.

When I chatted with Mom on the phone before the hearing date, I got the impression that she had no idea what was going on. Scott and I spoke several times before the hearing, and he assured me everything would turn out fine. Dan and I went ahead and made our reservations for flights, hotel, rental car. I packed a couple of business suits to wear to court.

Other than the group of relatives he was bringing to town, I had no idea what strategy Lenny had planned for this day-and-a-half hearing. Knowing my brother, I had seen that whenever he wanted to convince someone of an idea, he would argue with such authority that his listener couldn't help but buy whatever he was selling. Wielding his attorney credentials, Lenny had convinced our cousins on Mom's side that it was imperative to wrest guardianship away from Barbara Keithly. Poor Mom, he'd repeat, was being looked after by complete strangers who were only doing it in order to get hold of Mom's money. The solution lay in the hands of her loving family, who would be the saviors of their beloved Auntie Elise.

I was the only family member not in agreement with his idea; I believed Mom was doing as well as could be expected with Barbara as guardian. Mom would soon need round-the-clock supervision if she continued living in her home, and hiring qualified caregivers was expensive. Lenny's notion to move Mom to Rhode Island was not in Mom's interest, but it would be cheap. I knew that Mom dearly loved her church and circle of friends in Lakeland. The best I could do, then, was prevent Lenny from forcing Mom to move away.

Lenny persuaded our cousins to cooperate in his plan to bring Mom to Rhode Island where she would live with Aranoush. He urged them to think of all the money that would be saved! No more $60.00 an hour for the guardian, no more minimum wage for the lazy woman taking care of her. Plus, they could sell her house and keep all that money in reserve. The plan was foolproof. Lenny was sure there was no way they could lose, because he had looked up the relevant Florida laws, and the precedents were clear: The family must be given preference in guardianship.

He was in control. He directed his group of four family

members to get their plane tickets; that's all they would need. Once they landed in Tampa on October 25, they would all pile into a cheap rental van and drive over to Lakeland, where they would crash at Mom's place. Lenny had planned for the entourage to use the extra day before the hearing to remind Mom how much she loved them and how much she wanted to move to Rhode Island and live there.

The following day they would show up in court, and he'd call on them to testify. He rehearsed them to say how much they adored their Auntie Elise, who would be so much better off in the hands of her loving family in Cranston, Rhode Island. They need not worry about the traveling expenses—they would all be reimbursed once everything was turned over to Lenny and the family.

Let's take a closer look at the members of those in the traveling group, all making the trip to Lakeland, Florida, in order to take part in Lenny's plan.

Ara

The most senior member of the group was Ara, Mom's half-brother. In his eighties, he had recently retired from his job at a chemical manufacturing firm. Ara was a good-natured person, trusting and unassertive.

Aranoush

Next was Aranoush, Mom's half-sister, aged eighty. While she had immigrated from Syria to the U.S. in her twenties, she had remained closeted in the Rhode Island Armenian community and never acquired the education or skills to develop an informed view of the world. Her husband had passed away six months before our Florida hearing date. A stroke victim, John's last years had demanded a great deal of care. Aranoush had spent virtually all her waking hours taking care of him as best she could. But her best was inadequate since she was not well informed about his special needs. She fed him delicious Armenian meals and kept him and his surroundings clean. But she did not know that, when a person suffers a stroke, there exists only a brief window—around four hours—during which the stroke victim must be treated. Her lack of knowledge was painfully evident when, under her watch, John had suffered a stroke and fallen. She had allowed him to languish for several days afterward rather than call immediately for an ambulance. When one of her children came to the house and saw his condition, they'd finally taken him to the hospital. But by then, the window of time had long since elapsed and little could be done to help him recover.

A similar incident had taken place later, when John fell again. I'd heard Aranoush describe the severity of that fall, how very loud the thump had been. Again, she hadn't called for an ambulance, but several days later when he began complaining more insistently, their children had brought him to the hospital. The doctors determined that he had broken ribs in that fall. John developed pneumonia and never recovered.

One of my concerns about the feasibility of an elderly woman like Mom living in Aranoush's home was the fact that her apartment was on the second floor, accessible only via a steep flight of stairs in front and equally hazardous, unused stairs in back. Scaffolding remained standing in place, surrounding the run-down house for years, and a variety of rusted tools and hardware lay strewn in the back yard around that entrance.

Aranoush was a sweet, well-intentioned person, though hardly qualified to care for an acutely ill person. When I questioned her regarding her awareness of the special needs of an Alzheimer patient (such as my mother), she replied with confidence that she was fully aware, since she had read about it in *Readers Digest.*

Peter

The third person in the traveling group was Peter, Aranoush's eldest child, who was self-employed doing lawn maintenance and handyman jobs. Were he called to testify, he was prepared to state his availability as a driver. If Mom were living with Aranoush, and in the event she needed to be taken somewhere, he would be at the ready.

Peter is a great guy though not quite on top of things. His work ethic was exemplified in the state of disrepair of his mother's house. I saw the result of his idea to take parts of his church's dismantled chair lift and adapt them to function in Aranoush's back stairway. This idea never came to fruition; the cables and pieces of the old chair lift remained forever strewn along the hallway and stairs.

Rita

The fourth member of the traveling group was Rita, Aranoush's married daughter, who held a degree in Accounting. All I can say is, she should have known better. But I wasn't there when Lenny sold her, along with the rest of the group, his bill of goods. She once said, for example, that Lenny told her I was "stealing Mom's money." So when Rita was given a copy of Dan's spreadsheet detailing Mom's assets, she expressed astonishment to see that the holdings had steadily increased in value. But she had apparently sold her alliance to Lenny, and mere facts were not going to change her mind. Once Barbara Keithly had taken over as guardian, Lenny repeatedly expressed his fury at seeing Mom's money being frittered away by her, his personally chosen guardian. Rita had been the first to sign on to his campaign to get rid of spendthrift Barbara and move Mom to Rhode Island.

ON OCTOBER 9, 2003, LENNY SENT A LETTER TO Leroy Merkle, Barbara's attorney, informing him that they—he and his group of four—would be staying at Mom's place for the duration of the upcoming hearing. In addition, he informed Merkle that Aranoush would be staying with

Mom for at least an additional month, so there would be no need for a paid care-giver.

His fax to Merkle in part read:

> *This letter will serve as notification that myself, Elise's sister, her brother, and her niece and nephew Rita and Peter Yeretsian, plan to stay at Mom's home from October 25 through November 1. Her sister, Aranoush, plans on staying with Mom probably through Thanksgiving. . . . I object to your reference to the above family members as my 'traveling group,' and your characterization of Mom's family as 'angry people' who disrupt her daily and weekly routine.*

On October 17, Merkle filed a petition with the Court, with a copy sent to Lenny, prohibiting him and his traveling group from staying in Mom's home, and Aranoush from staying on later with Mom.

Merkle's letter stated that the guardian, Barbara Keithly, objected to Lenny and his traveling companions staying in Elise's residence, and that Barbara had previously advised him by letter that they "are welcome to visit their mother, but they must stay at another location while they are in town." In addition, he stated, Barbara Keithly, as guardian, was the person responsible for any decisions regarding Mrs. Yakoubian's care; the son, Lenny, was behaving in a manner that suggested his rights were superior to those of the guardian.

Lenny and his traveling group found a discount room at La Quinta Motel in Lakeland for their stay during the hearing.

14

THE HEARING

L ENNY HAD REQUESTED THIS HEARING for the primary purpose of obtaining permission to move Mom from Florida to Rhode Island. He also wanted to dismiss Barbara Keithly as Mom's legal guardian and replace her with one or more family members. The court determined that the second objective could not be addressed at this hearing.

The following people would take the stand and be questioned by both attorneys, Lenny representing himself, and Leroy Merkle representing Barbara:

- Ara Shiragian, Mom's brother
- Aranoush Yeretsian, Mom's sister
- Rita Yeretsian Marcotte, Aranoush's daughter
- Me

- Anita Rucker, Mom's friend, member of Lakeside Baptist
- Pixie Coleman, member of First Alliance Church
- Sherry Baker, Mom's former house-cleaner
- Asia Reid, Mom's caregiver

On October 27, 2003, my husband and I arrived at the Polk County Courthouse about half an hour before the hearing was scheduled to begin. A guard directed us to the blue elevators that would take us up to the ninth floor. The wood-paneled doors to our assigned courtroom were closed, so we sat on one of the chairs in the hallway. We had both dressed conservatively for the occasion, in dark business suits.

Dan was wondering about my Rhode Island relatives. He asked, "Are you going to talk to them when they show up? What are you going to say to them?"

My attitude at that point was annoyance verging on anger. I could only guess what Lenny could have said to persuade our relatives to participate in this exercise. I answered, "I'm going to ignore them. What could I possibly say that would be civil? I think they're idiots to fall for Lenny's BS."

Other people began arriving a few minutes later: my lawyer, Scott Langston, and Barbara, along with her lawyer. Then the Rhode Island group walked in together: Mom's brother and sister, Ara and Aranoush, and Aranoush's two children, Peter and Rita.

At 9:30, a guard emerged and motioned me to enter the courtroom. Dan and the four relatives had to remain outside. I walked in to find a room constructed almost entirely of wood—dark wood panels, creaky wood floors, pew-like wooden benches, and, in the center, a large judge's bench on a raised platform. Scott signaled me over to a seat on the right-hand side facing the judge's desk, several feet back. Barbara and her lawyer were seated in front of us. This is when I really started getting nervous. It was all so serious and official—I could think of a hundred other places I'd rather be that morning.

Looking around the room, I saw there was a uniformed guard seated off to the side of the judge's bench. Anyone who might be called to testify had to remain outside on the hallway seats.

The minutes ticked by—five, six, seven. . .ten. A door behind the judge's bench opened, and the judge entered. He was middle-aged, his hair cropped short, and he was wearing a black robe that resembled a choir robe. Everyone in the room rose the moment he came in. When he had taken his place at the bench, the guard indicated we could be seated.

Judge Herring looked us over, then tilted his head to question the guard. Sitting up straight again, he asked, "Is the plaintiff present?" Lenny was nowhere to be seen. Just as the judge was re-checking the time, the entrance door flew open and in trudged my brother, breathing heavily as if coming in from a foot race. Lenny has perennially been late for appointments, so his timing came as no big surprise. But one would have thought that, in this instance, where he had so much invested, he would have made the effort to arrive on time.

"I'm really sorry," he mumbled with an embarrassed grin. "The parking was impossible, I had to park a block away."

The guard indicated Lenny's assigned desk, to our left. He speed-shuffled his way forward, wearing heavy sports shoes and toting a lot of baggage. He shouldered off his jacket and huge backpack, which he unceremoniously dropped on the floor beside the desk.

Lenny had chosen to act as his own lawyer. Getting down to business, he retrieved a stack of folders from the backpack and proceeded to address the judge. He explained that he wished to get permission from the court to move Mom to Rhode Island, where she would live with and be cared for by her sister, Aranoush. He had brought witnesses, Mom's brother and sister as well as her niece and nephew, who were ready to testify in support of his proposal. He added that Aranoush's home would be safer and more comfortable for Mom, and that Aranoush was fully qualified to care for Mom. He called Ara Shiragian as the first witness.

Ara's Testimony

Responding to Lenny's question, Ara stated that, yes, he was educated, having earned a masters degree. He expressed full confidence in all aspects of Lenny's proposal. In response to a question regarding the means by which Mom could access Aranoush's apartment, he assured the court that, despite the fact that Aranoush's apartment was on the second floor and inaccessible, this posed absolutely no problem. How so? Ara explained, "Well, because there's a sort of escalator installed in the back stairway of the apartment, which Elise could ride up and down."

This was not true—no such thing existed. On my trip to Massachusetts and Rhode Island two weeks earlier, I had taken photos of the "sort of escalator," copies of which I had given to Scott. What existed there was a pile of dismantled pieces of an old chair lift that had once been in another building. Those random parts, along with miscellaneous cables and wires, were strewn on the unused back stairway of the apartment. By no stretch of the imagination could that stack of discarded segments ever be made to function on Aranoush's stairway. The stairs themselves were treacherous, poorly constructed, with treads only and no risers.

I wondered what making such a false statement said about Ara's concern for Mom's welfare. Perhaps he didn't care whether Mom would be housebound, unable to come and go as she wished. Or he was so taken in by Lenny's tale of Mom's money being squandered that he blindly trusted him to deal with the accessibility issue.

In response to Merkle's question concerning how

frequently he visited Mom in Florida, Ara stated that he visited her once— that is, one visit during the twenty-five years that she lived in Lakeland, if the visit ever actually took place.

Aranoush's Testimony

Aranoush is a cheerful, bright person though not well-informed—I doubted her ability to care for someone with advancing dementia. Her testimony in court was revealing. Replying honestly, she admitted that during Mom's fourteen-week extended stay in Rhode Island, they had arranged for several friends and family to take her out and about "more than ever before." She explained, "We never stayed home even for one day. We took her to the Roger Williams Park, we went to a big concert, we went many times to the church."

She didn't reveal that the reason for the unusual flurry of activity was to persuade Mom to change her mind about where she wished to live.

Rita's Testimony

Rita, the younger of Aranoush's two children, was in her late forties. She was married and had two young children. She had been an attractive young woman but had gained an inordinate amount of weight, making it hard to project a professional appearance. She was considered the more successful member of Aranoush's side of the family, having earned a degree in accounting. Rita's father, Aranoush's late husband, had had no education past high school. He had earned a living doing construction work in Cranston, but his workmanship was of mediocre quality—they had been barely able to make ends meet.

Lenny asked Rita several questions concerning Mom's happiness during the extended "vacation" she had recently spent in Rhode Island. He also posed questions pertaining to Aranoush's ability to care for Mom. Rita was enthusiastic in her responses, stating, "I saw Auntie Elise almost every day she was in Cranston. She really enjoyed every minute she was there. Auntie Elise was able to speak Armenian every day because she was always around other Armenians."

Rita went on to say, "She loved to cook with my mother. They made *kufta* and *lahmejoon* and other Armenian dishes that they don't even have the ingredients for in Florida."

Lenny asked whether she believed that Aranoush, at age eighty, was able to adequately care for Mom. Rita was equally enthusiastic in vouching for her mother's nursing capability. She referenced Aranoush's outstanding experience caring for her late husband following his two strokes. She neglected to mention the tragic result of Aranoush's lack of awareness of the window of time when a stroke victim must be treated in order to expect any recovery.

She also neglected to mention the deteriorating condition of Aranoush's house. A few years after these proceedings, Aranoush herself had to move out—the house would be sold at auction for $2,668.00.

The next person to testify was Sherry Baker, who had been Mom's house-cleaner for ten years, employed to help Mom shortly before my dad passed away in 1992. My parents had met her through friends at the Alliance church, where they had briefly attended before they switched to Lakeside Baptist. In my opinion, the Alliance church was more rigid and the members were known for their tendency to proselytize.

The Alliance "flavor" was frequently evident in Sherry Baker's conversation, especially when she spoke to people not of her church's denomination. Over the years, during the many times I visited my parents, it was a rare event when she didn't find the opportunity to quote a Bible verse or two. This sort of holier-than-thou posture is one reason why many people find evangelical Christians annoying.

As Sherry Baker took the stand at the Polk County courthouse, her piety was in full bloom. When Lenny asked her if she knew Elise's daughter, Mary Beth, she replied meekly, with head bowed, that yes, she did. Sherry then added, "Mary Beth didn't like me much. I don't know why she never liked me."

I should point out that I never had any strong feelings of like or dislike toward Sherry. I can only guess at the source of her antagonism. Under Lenny's questioning, she chose to condemn me on the witness stand, stating humbly under oath that I did not treat my mother well. A possible explanation for her resentment may have been that she believed I was responsible for her being terminated.

One of the questions that Leroy Merkle asked Sherry had to do with the form of payment she received for her work with Elise, whether it was in cash or by check. Sherry replied that it was both, sometimes one or sometimes the other. This was not true; she would accept cash only. Her first duty each Friday was to drive Mom to the bank and wait outside in the parking lot while Mom went in to withdraw the cash used to pay her.

The next witness was Anita Rucker, one of Mom's closest friends in Lakeland. Anita was around twelve years younger than Mom, placing her in her seventies. Anita kept in frequent touch with Mom, checking to see if she needed anything since Mom only got out once or twice a week. Anita was well aware of Lenny's attempts to control Mom's living arrangements and of his antagonistic behavior toward me. However, she was consistently tolerant and courteous in her interactions, never openly critical of him.

Anita was sworn in and took the stand. Merkle asked her questions about her relationship with Mom: how long they had known each other, how often they spoke, and so forth. He then asked Anita to describe her observation of the mother–daughter relationship and specific conversations she may have witnessed. Anita replied in detail, describing some specific examples of the happiness Mom expressed at having me around. She added that she thought it was amusing when she and Mom went shopping together—Mom would delay making purchases till I was there visiting, as she knew I would buy her whatever she needed.

Lenny asked Anita a few questions as well, coming straight to the point concerning Mom's present situation.

"In your conversations with Elise, have you discussed with her whether she is content with her present living conditions here in Lakeland?"

"Yes, sometimes."

"Has she told you where she prefers to be, here or with her family in Rhode Island?"

"No, I don't think so."

Lenny asked Anita questions pertaining to the antagonism between me (as Elise's daughter) and himself, to which she could have had a lot to say, but she held back and avoided saying anything critical. Lenny thanked her.

Lenny called me next. Scott gave my hand a reassuring squeeze as I walked forward to take the witness stand. Lenny's first question to me had to do with a lengthy email he had sent me several months earlier. He simply couldn't understand why I had never replied to his important message. He held a copy in his hand and placed the pages on the railing of the witness stand directly in front of me. Despite comforting assurances from my lawyer, I was pretty nervous about being in that awkward situation. And I had become angrier by the minute, sitting there and watching the spectacle Lenny was conducting. I looked at those pages lying on the rail in front of me and wanted badly to pick them up and rip them into pieces. I bit my tongue and said nothing.

When I first received that message at home, I had started to read it. But I quickly realized that, number one, it was really long—several pages long—and number two, there was absolutely no way I was going to reply to it. Clearly, whatever it said, Lenny was in the right, as always, and anything I had to say would be a total waste of time. I chose not to continue reading the message.

Lenny again insisted that I answer him, but my lawyer objected and the judge directed Lenny to move on. He then asked me what plans I visualized for Mom.

I explained, "Mom's name was on the waiting list of Presbyterian Homes for years. When her name eventually came up for an independent living apartment there, it happened to be right about the same time that her doctor had advised that she be moved somewhere with supervision available. We had visited the Presbyterian Homes community and found it to be ideal."

Lenny interrupted, "How much was it going to cost?" True to form, he was boiling everything down to dollars and cents.

I replied, "The initiation fee was fifty-four thousand dollars. Then you pay a monthly fee for the apartment and meals. When Mom could no longer get along on her own in the 'independent living' apartment, she would then be eligible to move over to one of the assisted living units." I went into a little more detail about the structure of a progressive care community such as Presbyterian Homes. I noted that, in addition to its superior reputation, Presbyterian had the advantage of being nearby and currently housed several people Mom knew at Lakeside Baptist.

Question: "Where is the fifty-four thousand dollars?"

"The payment was never made, since Mom didn't get the apartment."

"What happened to the fifty-four thousand dollars?"

At first I couldn't follow what he was trying to get at. Then I realized he wanted to make it look like I'd kept the money for myself.

"If you check Barbara Keithly's annual accounting, you'll find the fifty-four thousand dollars. When I turned over Mom's records, it was still in the same account at the same bank. Not paid."

Lenny looked like he wanted to pursue this line further, but had run out of ideas. He paused and started smirking at this point, warming up to ask the next question. He must have believed he had uncovered a piece of damning information which he was about to spring.

"Did you have people lined up to rent the house after Mom moved out?"

"I assume you're referring to Bryan and Michele Sasser."

His smirk grew into a wide grin as if he'd just outed a big secret. "So they were going to live in Mom's house after she was gone?"

"Right. They're a young couple from Mom's church, and were aware the rental might be temporary. Mom was going to try Presbyterian Homes for two months. If she liked it, she would stay there, and if she didn't, then she would go back to the house."

I should have added that Presbyterian was very accommodating to allow Mom to move in on a trial basis. I believed she would love it, but they had given us the option of moving out if Mom was not happy there.

The grin disappeared—not a huge coup after all. Lenny had lost interest in that line of questioning. He shuffled the papers he was holding, then went on to ask what was my "Plan B." At that point, my lawyer got up and objected—he felt the question had already been answered. The judge agreed.

Lenny did more paper shuffling, then asked: "Did you ever ask Mom if she would like to live in Providence?"

"Yes, I did."

"What was her answer?"

"She said, 'Oh, no! Never, never, never!'"

Lenny wasn't happy with that answer: "No further questions."

I was permitted to step down.

Lenny also called Pixie Coleman and Asia Reid to testify. Both of them were brief and said little that I can remember. I believe Pixie met Mom through Sherry Baker, as both were members of the Alliance church. She had known Mom for a relatively short period of time. Asia, Mom's caregiver at the time, was uncharacteristically reticent and said nothing of interest.

What followed was Lenny's own testimony. It was a long, rambling recitation, some parts completely irrelevant. He described my parents' history, starting with their life in Connecticut through their subsequent move to Florida. He explained that the primary reason for their moving away had been to escape from their other son, David, who had serious emotional issues. David's belligerent episodes made life for them nerve-wracking, especially for Mom. Lenny continued to describe Mom's docile personality, always dependent on Dad and still dependent on others.

Switching gears, Lenny decided it was time to talk about how poor Barbara had been as guardian. The worst thing she had done, in his opinion, was to hire an irresponsible caregiver who had nearly caused Mom to have a nervous breakdown. He went into graphic detail, talking about the time when Mom was in Rhode Island shortly after Sandra Meyer's dismissal. She was having hallucinations, terrified, imagining wild horses were coming after her.

Lenny finally turned his attention to Mom's likes and dislikes, expressing his concern that her wishes be taken into consideration. He explained that Mom was happiest when she was among her relatives in Rhode Island. He was sure, he continued, that Mom would much prefer to live there rather than in Florida.

At this point, my lawyer interjected that Lenny could not read Mrs. Yakoubian's mind, and that she should be allowed to speak for herself. The judge agreed with Scott's assertion but felt it would be upsetting for Mom to take the stand and be questioned. He recommended that he meet with Mom himself, one on one, and ask her directly what her wishes were. There were a number of small rooms available in the building where she and the judge could sit comfortably and talk informally. The meeting would be televised on closed circuit TV and transmitted to another room in the building, where we would be able to watch. This proposal was agreed to by everyone.

Since it was nearly 5:00, the judge was ready to adjourn for the day. He directed Barbara to see that Mrs. Yakoubian was brought to the courthouse the next morning, at which time the hearing would resume.

Friday morning, we were all back, seated in exactly the same places. The judge opened with some formalities, then repeated the recommendation he had made for Mom to be brought in for a private meeting with him. We all agreed to the logistics he laid out.

Asia, who was still employed at the time, was waiting with Mom—the guard left to assist her in bringing Mom to the designated room. All of us in the courtroom were led to a viewing room to watch the judge's discussion with Mom. The room was located on an upper floor in the court building, an area that required the six of us to first parade through a large open office full of busy clerical workers.

The viewing room turned out to be a large meeting room, furnished with a long conference table in the center and additional seating arranged along the walls surrounding the table. There were two large TV monitors, one on the wall at the far end of the room, the other suspended from the ceiling in the center, directly above the conference table. Both were tuned in to a close-up view of a small room where two upholstered chairs stood close to each other. There seemed to be a problem with the hanging TV—the picture was full of static and kept blinking while the other was working fine.

Lenny decided to come to the rescue. He jumped on the table, reached up and began fiddling with the TV knobs. A few seconds of that, and the TV stopped functioning altogether. So our only view would be the one TV on the wall. We took our seats and watched the screen, which in a few minutes showed the judge and Mom as they entered the small room and sat in the upholstered chairs.

The judge introduced himself and shook hands with Mom. He chatted with her casually for a while, apparently to make Mom feel more comfortable in the odd situation. After a few minutes, she adjusted herself in the chair and flashed the judge a big smile. Apparently his gentle demeanor had been successful in getting her to relax.

The judge asked, "Was that your aide I saw sitting next to you in the waiting room?"

"Yes, that's right."

"I didn't have a chance to talk to her. How is she doing? Are you satisfied with her care?"

"Yes, she's good."

"And how about your guardian—you don't see her as often. How do you feel about her?"

"She's very nice. I like her."

He paused and then asked, "Do you understand why we are having this meeting today?"

She hesitated and replied, "Yes, I think so."

"You know, then, that many people, including your family, are very concerned about your well-being."

"Yes, I do."

"Now, my job is to listen to what everyone has to say and figure out what's really best for you. Not everyone is in agreement, so I have to weigh the pros and cons before I come to a conclusion."

"Um-hmm."

"The main question that needs to be answered is where you will live from now on. That's a pretty important question, so we need to consider all sides carefully in order to find the best answer."

"Yes, that's true."

"Mrs. Yakoubian, I hope you can tell me honestly what

your wishes are. I believe this question is a difficult, serious one. Promise you'll think very carefully before you answer."

"Yes, I will do my best."

"Now, if you had to make a choice today, how would you choose? Would you want to go to Rhode Island and live with your sister, Aranoush? Or would you prefer to live here in Lakeland, Florida?"

"Hmmm. It's a very hard question."

"It *is* a hard question. Please take your time and think carefully."

There was a lengthy pause. "Well, to tell you the truth," she finally said, "my answer is to stay in Lakeland."

The judge leaned forward and rested a hand on Mom's hand. "I know this is stressful for you. But you are sure now that your choice is to live here in Lakeland?"

"Yes, I would like to stay here."

The judge smiled and patted her hand. "Thank you for being so patient. And thank you for making your wishes clear. Let me get your aide now to take you back to the waiting room. Good-bye, Mrs. Yakoubian."

"Good-bye, sir."

Everyone in the TV viewing room exhaled in relief at the conclusion of the meeting. Everyone except Lenny, of course. We all trooped through the office full of clerks, back to the courtroom.

We took our seats and waited for the judge to return. As

the rear entrance door opened and the judge entered the room, Lenny rushed over from the side and began gesticulating and speaking urgently to the judge. Every one of us turned and stared, not quite believing what was happening. Lenny had absolutely no right to confront the judge anywhere except in the specified confines of the courtroom. This scene went on for a couple of minutes, and then the judge abruptly cut Lenny off and strode forward to the bench.

We soon learned what that was all about: The judge allowed Lenny to state his argument before all of us. He was in a highly agitated state: "She should have been asked who she wants to make decisions for her. The second question was not addressed. Mrs. Yakoubian should be asked to decide if she wants to terminate Barbara as her legal guardian. She should have been asked who she prefers to make decisions for her."

The judge cut him off. "The question is not on the agenda."

Lenny's voice rose in pitch: "But with all due respect, I asked to have the guardianship question added."

"There are no further motions presented. It's time to conclude."

The old habit of stamping his foot and repeating his demands may have served Lenny well in getting his way as a child, but it did nothing to advance his cause in the courtroom. I suspect it further alienated the judge, who, of course, had to decide the case.

"I have another witness with critical testimony. Peter Yeretsian traveled here at huge expense to make a statement."

"The time is now 11:30. You can either close now or carry over till Monday morning. What is your choice?"

"They can't! They can't stay till Monday."

"What do you want to do?"

There was another pause before Lenny said, "We'll close."

With that, the hearing ended.

A few minutes later, everyone concerned met in the hall outside the courtroom to say their good-byes. Waiting there were the Rhode Island family members and my husband with Mom's friend Betsy Cable, who had arrived late. Mom and Asia had found their way to the hall and were sitting together. I crouched down next to Mom and told her it was over—she didn't have to come back there anymore.

"What's going to happen?"

"Don't worry, Mom, it's all settled. The judge said you can stay here in Lakeland."

The judge had said no such thing, but it was pretty obvious what the outcome would be. She got up, threw her arms around me, and gave me a giant hug. She patted my face and said, "You look so pretty. You changed your hair!"

That was her way of saying, "Thank you, Mary."

15

LANETTE

DAN AND I CHECKED OUT of the Holiday Inn and returned to New Jersey the next day; I was relieved the hearing was over and hoped maybe I'd be able to sleep better.

That two-day hearing in October 2003 was a stunning failure for Lenny, after he had spent so much time, energy, even money to get what he wanted. Judge Herring wouldn't send out the written ruling till several weeks afterward, but how he would ultimately rule should have been obvious. The closed-circuit interview he'd had with my mother clinched the deal. There wasn't much chance he would rule in Lenny's favor after Mom clearly expressed her wish to remain living in Lakeland.

In addition to Mom's oral statement, there was on record a copy of her written statement dated October 7, 2003:

I, Elise Yakoubian, hereby declare that Florida is my home and I do not want to leave for any reason to move to Providence, Rhode Island. I have a home and I'm comfortable. I would like to go visit once a year but it is too cold! I do not want to move from my house and that is fact. What would I do with my beautiful things. I have no reason to move. Is that foolish to want to stay in my own home. I do not want to sell my house. I will never sell my house. I want to live in my own home. Everything has been going smoothly. I don't want any changes. Leon said don't ever sell the house.

I asked Barbara Keithly to write my words down for me.

(Signed), Elise Yakoubian

Despite Mom's clear response to the Judge during their interview, Lenny refused to accept her answer. A few weeks after the hearing, on November 26, he sent a lengthy closing argument to Judge Herring in which he repeated the same arguments made in court. These included:

- Mom's response to the Judge should be given little weight because she "is an adjudicated incompetent."
- The interview did not provide reliable evidence of her desires.

- The guardian's performance has been inadequate and costly.
- The written statement is not in Mom's handwriting.
- The written statement does not reflect Mom's feelings.
- Mom is unhappy with the Guardian for a variety of reasons.
- It is very costly to have the Guardian provide care for Mom.
- Moving to Rhode Island offers several benefits for Mom, such as her living expenses would be reduced significantly.
- Mom has made it clear that she wants to go to Rhode Island.

On December 5, 2003, Judge Herring issued his "Order of the Court" in which he ruled in favor of Barbara Keithly. I learned later that Judge Herring had said privately to an attorney familiar with the case, "There's no way on Earth I would grant guardianship to that guy." I had to smile when I heard that.

Barbara fired Asia in the summer of 2004, after the candle incident. In order to find a replacement, Barbara placed a help wanted ad in the *Lakeland Ledger*. She couldn't offer more in the way of salary, since Mom's funds were being rapidly depleted. Barbara's fee as guardian, her assistant Nancy's salary and travel expenses, Barbara's lawyer's fee, the cost of weekly groceries, and the salary of a full-time caregiver were eating up Mom's balance.

Barbara felt that by including the offer of room and board, in addition to the minimum-wage salary, she could attract a capable person to be Mom's live-in caregiver. She interviewed several applicants and found Lanette Dees far and away the best qualified. Lanette was young, just thirty-six years old, had completed two years at a local community college and had several years' experience as a live-in nanny for two young children. Although she had no experience caring for the elderly, Barbara felt the excellent recommendation from her previous employer made up for it. Lanette's prior position had been in southern Florida, though she was in fact a native of Lakeland, where her mother and stepfather still lived.

Two weeks after Asia's termination, Lanette Dees moved her belongings into the guest bedroom in Mom's house. It was love at first sight—Mom and Lanette hit it off instantly. Lanette needed a stable place to live, and Mom needed someone with her who was genuinely caring and willing to spend time just talking.

During the two years that Asia had looked after Mom, they rarely talked more than was absolutely necessary. Asia had apparently spent a lot of time on her phone or watching TV. This became clear after a number of calls with Mom when I asked her about Asia's work and what she and Asia talked about. She replied that they didn't have time to talk as Asia was always busy in some other room or on the phone with her son.

When I was at the house visiting Mom and observed their interaction, Asia would make a point of speaking playfully to her—I wonder if maybe she did so just for my benefit. Partly because of Asia's regional accent, I could see that Mom had understood little of what she said. One of my favorites took place one day when Mom was nicely dressed, ready for us to go visiting friends, and Asia declared: "Miz Leese, you be lookin good fo' da mins!"

Mom looked at me and asked, "*Eench ge-seh gor?*" Translation: "What is she saying?"

I said, "Asia wants you to have a good time when we go out."

Lanette was a welcome contrast; she doted on Mom all day, every day. Over the course of a few conversations I had with her, I learned from her that she had experienced trauma in her teens. She explained that she had been exploited by a relative and had not completely gotten over it. That hurt may partly have accounted for her being so needy and receptive to Mom's sincere show of affection. As Mom was an earnest listener, they were perfect foils for each other, each satisfying the other's needs. Whenever Lanette told other people about her work with Mom, she would invariably say, "She changed my life." That may have been a little hyperbolic, but it was clear that Lanette had found compassion and understanding with my Mom. And nothing could make Mom feel happier than when she was able to make someone else happy.

Lanette was tall and slender, with long blond hair and a ready, sweet smile. She had no trouble attracting men, though the men she had been seeing didn't seem to be the best. Not long after moving in with Mom, she found a new boyfriend, one who had a lot more going for him. Perhaps it was the genuine friendship she shared with Mom that was proving to be a stabilizing influence. Lanette was also a proficient cook. From the very first, she prepared three well-balanced meals daily, which she and Mom sat down and had together.

I had talked to Lanette on the phone before meeting her in person. I found her to be forthcoming in telling me exactly how Mom was doing, and I was happy to answer questions about Mom that might be useful for her to know. Of course, we talked about Asia and the problems leading to her dismissal. We discovered later that Mom's gold jewelry was missing, but many people had been in and out of the house, and there was no way to prove who took it, so I just chalked it up to experience. Lanette told me about one incident that demonstrated Asia's entitled attitude. It happened just a few days after Lanette started working at Mom's. Asia showed up at the door. She had come for spices. She informed Lanette that she wanted to take the spices from the pantry. Lanette was taken aback. She politely declined, informing Asia that, sorry, she would be needing to use the spices herself. It was such a brazen move, almost laughable.

Lanette was pretty adept at juggling questions posed by Mom's three children. With David, who called occasionally when he wasn't high, she would just make small talk. Lenny would call more frequently and try to elicit information from her about Mom's interaction with me. He and Lanette met in person earlier in her employment than I did, when he'd gone to visit Mom. Lenny can be quite charming—he and Lanette hit it off in in a way that I could not. The one topic about which he talked to her often, during his visit as well as during phone calls, involved his plan to have Mom make another trip to Rhode Island to visit her sister's family.

Lenny's focus was still on the money. He fought Barbara's every move in court, filing objections to each and every expense. While he did not object specifically to payments made to Lanette, he was still contriving a way to eliminate the expense of having a paid caregiver at all, which was a big chunk of Mom's budget. Nearly a year had elapsed since the hearing and his failed attempt to relocate Mom up north. It became clear that he still had not given up on his idea of moving her to Rhode Island.

I wonder if Lenny may have been a tiny bit embarrassed at having lost the court case so badly, after promising his entourage that he would surely prevail. He had a variety of excuses for losing, among them being that the court had been biased against him. "The Florida law was crystal clear: I should have been granted guardianship of Mom— the judge's interpretation was wrong!"

Lanette had begun as Mom's caregiver several months after the hearing. She and Mom had quickly become best buddies. Mom's ninety-first birthday had just passed, and I decided to have a party for her at the house. Over the phone, I enrolled Lanette and Michelle Sasser to help plan the event. I had given Mom a big bash at the church hall the previous year for her ninetieth, but since Mom had been growing weaker, I felt it would be best to do it at home this time.

The day after I got to Lakeland, I went through Mom's closet to pick a suitable dress for her party. I found a couple of OK ones, but they were all pretty old.

I said to Lanette, "How about we go to the mall and get Mom a new dress for the party?"

"How about it! That's a great idea."

"Let's do it. It's got to be special—you're only ninety-one once."

"That's funny. If you ever get there at all."

We decided to drive over after dinner. We went straight to Belk, where they would have a wide selection. It didn't take us long to boil our choices down to three dresses.

I said, "Let's just get all three. Whatever doesn't fit, I'll return next week."

"Perfect! Your mom will love to have a choice."

Back home, before our midnight snack and tea (at 9:00 p.m.), we showed Mom the dresses.

Lanette said, "C'mon, Elise, we need to pick a dress for your birthday party."

"Birthday party? But it's not my birthday."

"It's always a good time to have a party. Look at this rose-colored one—it's my favorite."

"Oh, what a pretty color."

Mom tried on all three dresses; she wound up agreeing on the rose-colored one. It was a good length—I didn't even have to hem it.

There was a Party City outlet at the Grove Park Mall. I went there and bought out the place—decorations, matching colored plates, napkins—the works.

We had sent invitations and also had an announcement about the event in the church bulletin. On the day of the party, Lanette dressed Mom in her new rose-colored dress and sat her like a movie star at the head of the living room. She looked better than she had in years. Her hair had turned completely silver, and her new perm made a perky frame around her smiling face.

It was a bright sunshiny day, and many friends from Lakeside Baptist came to wish her a happy birthday. Barbara and Nancy made the trip from Tampa to join in the celebration. While guests stopped by her side to chat, I took a lot of photos so I could put together an album for her. She absolutely loved to browse through the album of the previous year's party. Though her memory had continued to gradually decline, Mom enjoyed herself in the moment.

The Grove Park Deli had provided lavishly arranged platters of hors d'oeuvres and a sheet cake decorated with butter-cream orange and lavender flowers and an inscription that read *Happy Birthday, Elise.* Guests milled around and admired Mom's unusual decorative pieces, such as the intricate Armenian needle-lace doily that we'd had framed and that hung on the living room wall. Another eye-catching piece was a tapestry throw I'd given Mom for Christmas 1999. The inscription read *Armenian Christianity 1700 Anniversary,* and woven in were images of Armenian saints and holy sites. Mom loved that tapestry and kept it on display across the back of her long sofa. One of the guests, Chuck DeBats, helped me hold the tapestry up at either end so people could see the entire pattern. The design around the border included the Armenian alphabet, which Mom read aloud for her guests. One of them asked, "Elise, where did you get this?"

She hesitated, then smiled and explained, "That's a very special piece that was given to me a long time ago."

Another guest, who happened to know its history, asked, "What a beautiful gift. Who gave it to you?"

That was the limit of Mom's hedging. She admitted, "Well, I don't remember exactly, but I've had it now for many years."

I probably shouldn't have said anything, but I did feel

disappointed that she'd forgotten about a gift I'd jumped through hoops to get for her. I said, "Mom, I think I gave you that, didn't I?"

She smiled tentatively, "Yes, that's right! It's from Mary."

16

DEATH TRIP

URING THE SPRING OF 2004, LENNY HAD BEGUN a new campaign to send Mom off to Rhode Island for another "vacation." It included a barrage of faxed letters, phone calls, and emails to Barbara and later to Judge Herring as well.

Since Mom's care was under the supervision of a legal guardian, she was not permitted, by law, to leave the state without Barbara Keithly's express permission. Barbara was not inclined to allow any more trips, since Mom's health was in decline. She had become weaker and often needed to use a walker when she went out. Barbara informed Lenny that Mom had suffered a "spell" and couldn't get out of the tub. She'd had to call Hugh Johnson to the house to help. Nancy had taken her to Dr. Hix at Watson Clinic; Mom hadn't been able to walk from the car to the entrance and had to use a wheelchair.

By that time, I saw it would be unwise for her to consider a plane trip anywhere. I learned about what Lenny was planning through conversations with Barbara. She tried to be even-handed in dealing with us, taking both our views into consideration. Prior to the October 2003 hearing, there had been much more communication between Barbara and Lenny than between Barbara and me. He had, after all, been the one to select her as Mom's guardian, through his lawyer's recommendation. And in all probability, he had bad-mouthed me to Barbara. Once the outcome of the hearing was said and done, Barbara understood that I was not the bogey-man Lenny had apparently made me out to be.

Around the middle of June, I heard from Barbara that Lenny had become adamant in pressing her for permission to allow Mom to go to Rhode Island. I couldn't believe it. She had advised him Mom was weaker—why would he want to subject her to the stress of traveling? Barbara and I discussed it and agreed it was a foolish idea. "MB, how does Elise look to you? How do you think she might cope with a trip to Providence?"

"Barbara, I just saw my mother last month. There's no way she's up to traveling."

"I believe you're right. Nancy just took her back to see Dr. Hix for an evaluation."

"She did? So what did he say?"

"He said what we already know. He advised against a trip."

"Did he put it in writing?"

"He will. His office is going to send me a copy."

Dr. Hix advised against it, but his recommendation didn't deter Lenny—he continued to insist that Mom be sent to Providence again. On July 5, Lenny faxed the following to Barbara, with a copy to Judge Herring:

Dear Barbara:

I am writing in response to your letter of July 2, 2004, in which you declined to allow Mom to visit her extended family in Providence, RI. . . . Your letter stated, "Elise is 91 years old and no longer able to travel for family gatherings."

I have taken some time to think about your position, and to consult with family members, and have prepared the following response, which is sent with the approval of Mom's sister, brother, her only two grandchildren, her two sons, and her niece and nephew. As you well know, these are, all of Mom's blood relatives, except for one, her daughter, Mary.

Speaking for the family, we are extremely upset that for the second time since the hearing on Mom's custody in October, you have used your authority to prevent Mom from visiting her family. . . .

It appears clear that Mom is able to travel to the

airport, board and sit on a three-hour flight, and then be taken care of by her closest family members in their home for two or three weeks. Her current daily activities in Lakeland involve as much or more travel, visiting, and sitting than will be involved in the proposed trip to spend time with her family in Providence. Aside from Mom's short-term memory loss, gradually declining mobility and energy, and emotional upset over her situation, Mom's condition appears quite stable.

Mom herself repeatedly asks when she will be allowed to visit her family in Providence. . . .

On behalf of her family, I request that you reconsider your decision and inform me in writing within one week. Please be advised that the family has decided that, in the event that you maintain your position, we will request that the court address this issue.

Sincerely,

While all this letter-writing was going on, I continued to talk to Mom on the phone regularly. During one call that July, I asked if she was thinking about going on a trip to Providence; she hesitated, sounding mystified about why I would ask such a question. She said she had just gone there recently and had no reason to go back. I thought I'd question Mom a bit further—perhaps I could jog her memory about a conversation she may have had with Lenny.

"Well, Aranoush always loves to see you. If she invited you, do you think you'd like to go?"

"*Anoushig,* how should I answer? If I don't go, do you think their feelings will be hurt?"

"No, Mom, I don't think so."

Unbelievable! So Mom really had no desire to travel to Rhode Island, but she imagined their feelings would be hurt if she declined. It was so like her, always wishing to please others, even when it was to her own detriment.

She then changed the subject and asked when I would be coming to Florida to see her. She asked me this question every time I talked to her, and I usually replied that it would probably be in a few weeks. That answer seemed to satisfy her. After chatting a little longer, I was convinced Mom was not "repeatedly asking to be allowed to visit her family in Providence." Whether or not she was physically able to make the trip was a question for Dr. Hix.

If I had to speculate on that conversation Lenny had had with Mom, I've no doubt it included questions like, "Wouldn't you like to go and see Aranoush and Ara?" Of course she would never say "no" to any such question. But I clearly recall how confused Mom had been after returning from her fourteen-week "long vacation" in Providence a year earlier. She couldn't understand why it had gone on for so long, and she remembered hardly anything that happened while she was there.

On July 5, the same day as his three-page letter to Barbara, Lenny drafted another letter to Barbara for our relatives—five people—to sign:

Dear Barbara,

We were quite disappointed and dismayed to learn that you have denied Elise the right to visit us this summer or any time thereafter. You state that Elise is 91 years old and can no longer travel. These days, air travel is no more than an extended car ride. . . .

Also, you stated that the family is more than welcome to travel to Florida and visit with Elise in her home while making overnight arrangements elsewhere. When Elise visits, we plan several family gatherings which include relatives from Massachusetts, Connecticut, New York, New Jersey, Virginia and California. She thoroughly enjoys attending the Armenian Church, participating in the preparation of her favorite Armenian delicacies, visiting with her cherished relatives and dear long-time friends, and reminiscing about the past. . . . We could not possibly create the same warm family environment while staying in an area hotel.

Therefore we respectfully ask that you reconsider your decision to terminate any current and/or future plans for Elise to visit her brother, sister, chil-

dren, grandchildren, nieces, nephews and numerous
cousins. . . .

> *Very truly yours,*
> *Ara Shiragian (brother)*
> *Aranoosh V. Yeretsian (sister)*
> *Peter Yeretsian (nephew)*
> *Rita Yeretsian Marcotte (niece)*
> *Grace Shiragian (niece)*
> *Cc: Judge Herring*

On July 13, Barbara faxed Lenny a letter again denying his request. In it, she explained the reasons why it would be a mistake to send Mom on a trip at that time:

Dear Lenny:

> *This is a follow-up to your past letter and*
> *another family letter. I understand you're upset that*
> *your mom can no longer do the things she has done*
> *for the past 40 years, but I believe you are in total*
> *denial as to your mom's capabilities. However, I*
> *take exception to your likening flying to an ex-*
> *tended car trip. It is much more tiring having to*
> *travel by car to the airport in Tampa, walk to tick-*
> *eting, ride in a wheelchair to the gate, the 3-hour*
> *flight, more riding, etc., etc. Add to this the con-*
> *fusion of being away from home with advanced*
> *Alzheimer's. You also should know that Elise is*

now having incontinent episodes and begun using
Depends. Elise cannot even walk from the car into
Watson Clinic at this point. Nancy has to take the
wheelchair and wheel her in to appointments.

I appreciate the importance of family and family
gatherings, but in this instance, you will need to
come to Florida.

Sincerely,

When Lenny didn't receive his desired response by July
14, he faxed a twenty-five-page letter to Judge Herring
(three new pages and twenty-two copies of previous corre-
spondence), requesting him to intervene and compel Barbara to allow Mom to make the trip.

Dear Judge Herring:
I am writing to request that you review the deci-
sion of my Mother's guardian, Barbara Keithly, to
deny the request of Mom's family, and Mom, to
spend two to three weeks with the family at their
home in Providence, Rhode Island. I am making
this request on behalf of Mom's sister, brother, her
only two grandchildren, her two sons, and her niece
and nephew - all of Mom's family with the excep-
tion of her daughter Mary (the "Family"). . . .
Your Honor. . . . The fact that Mom has occa-
sional incontinent episodes and uses "Depends"

does not make this travel unreasonably difficult. The very purpose of "Depends" is to permit a person to be secure despite a delay in getting to the bathroom. . . .

I am concerned and request that your Honor consider the possibility that the Guardian is being unduly influenced by Mary Yakoubian, who has estranged herself from Mom's family and has spared no efforts to limit Mom's involvement with her family. Mary has repeatedly sought to assert unilateral control over Mom, without regard for or consultation with other family members. I am also concerned and request that Honor consider the possibility that the Guardian is hostile to Mom's family because they criticized the Guardian's performance and sought to terminate the Guardian's custody of Mom at the October hearing. At that hearing the only family member that argued in favor of retaining the Guardian was Mary Yakoubian. . . .

On behalf of the family, I request that you direct the Guardian to permit and cooperate in the proposed and future visits. Should a hearing be appropriate, I request that it be telephonic, in order that it contain costs and provide an equal opportunity for all interested parties to participate. Should the Guardian seek to introduce any doctor's statements or other materials in support of her position,

I request your Honor require such materials be pro-
vided to all parties at least three days in advance of
any hearing. . . .

    Respectfully submitted,

It's impossible to describe my reaction to reading this letter, which I saw as the ultimate in irony when Lenny paints me as "sparing no efforts to limit Mom's involvement with her family," and "repeatedly seeking to assert unilateral control over Mom." In reality, the hundreds of pages on record show Lenny sparing no effort to compel Mom to bend to his wishes and leave Florida against her will. This letter was addressed to Judge Herring, the same judge who had presided at the October hearing and had been exasperated by Lenny's similar language then.

Presumably to further bolster his position, Lenny had attached to this message the additional twenty-two pages of copies: letters from him to Barbara, from Barbara to him, from the "family" to Barbara, and to the judge.

A week later, when Lenny had not received a reply to this message, he faxed the judge an "urgent request":

Dear Judge Herring:

    I am writing to request that you take action this
week on the request made on behalf of the Ward's
family (her sister, brother, her only two grandchil-

dren, her two sons, and her niece and nephew),
made on July 14, 2004, to review the decision of my
Mother's guardian, Barbara Keithly, to deny the
request of Mom's family, and Mom, to spend two
or three weeks with the family at their home in
Providence, Rhode Island.

By my letter of July 14, the family requested that
you direct the Guardian to permit and cooperate in
the proposed and future visits. As noted in the letter,
we have been trying to arrange this visit since last
Christmas, and it is urgent that we complete plans
in order to get the family and Mom together before
summer vacation is over. Thus, your action on this
matter this week is urgently requested.

Respectfully submitted,

On July 26, Lenny got his answer via fax, in which the
judge consented to holding a hearing on the matter:

Dear Mr. Yakoubian:
The Court is in receipt of your faxed transmis-
sions of July 14 and July 21, 2004.... If you wish
to schedule this for a hearing, you may contact this
office to obtain hearing date(s) and time(s). Please
note that any hearing date must be cleared with all
parties before it will be scheduled on the Court's cal-
endar.

Sincerely,
Ronald A. Herring
Chief Judge

It's a mystery how Lenny could possibly have been un-aware of the negative impression he had made on Judge Herring in October, when he had unequivocally ruled against Lenny and in favor of Barbara. At the end, the judge's irritation with Lenny's performance was evident in the very tone of his voice as he summarily closed the hearing.

The idea of another hearing did not sit well with Lenny, as was made clear by the next action he took. In a last-ditch effort to sway Barbara, he recruited Mom's sister, Aranoush, to appeal to Barbara. Mom's eighty-year-old sister again dutifully agreed to follow his directions. He gave her Barbara's phone number and a list of talking points to appeal to her directly. The fact that Aranoush's call was not spontaneous was obvious in her choice of words requesting Barbara's permission, repeating the exact terminology regularly used by Lenny. Aranoush's accented English may not have been perfect, but her sincerity was perfectly convincing. Her plea, added to the prospect of another hearing, proved to be the last straw for Barbara. She caved and reversed her decision, granting permission for Mom to make the trip to Rhode Island in August.

August 5 saw Lenny's last fax to Judge Herring, in

which he withdrew his hearing request and acknowledged Aranoush's role in obtaining Barbara's reversal:

> *Dear Judge Herring:*
>
> *I am writing to withdraw the request for a hearing.* . . .
>
> *As the Guardian has agreed with the Ward's sister, Aranoush Yeretsian, to permit the planned visit, there no longer is a reason for requesting the hearing.*
>
> *Respectfully submitted,*

Mom couldn't pack for herself, so the evening before her departure, Lanette packed a suitcase for her as best she could. It was a steamy morning in August 2004 when Nancy arrived to pick Mom up and drive her to Tampa Airport. Lanette and Nancy walked her to Nancy's car, all the while reminding her that it would be only a few weeks, and then she would be coming right back home. Yes, they assured Mom, Lanette would still be there waiting for her.

Once they were on the road, rolling along I-4, Mom cheered up—she still loved to go for rides. Nancy later told me how, many times during that drive, Mom asked her where they were going. Each time Nancy replied they were going to go on a plane trip to Providence to visit Mom's sister. Each time Mom's reply was a simple, "Oh."

At the airport, an airline attendant rolled over a wheelchair for Mom, but she refused initially to use it. "I can walk by myself," she said.

Nancy and the attendant exchanged tolerant smiles. Nancy leaned toward Mom and stage-whispered, "Of course, I know you can. But if you ride in a wheelchair, they'll let us board the plane first. Get it?"

Mom giggled, tickled to be in on the ploy, then went ahead and sat herself down in the chair. Nancy explained to Mom not to worry, that she would be sitting on the plane with her. This perked Mom up, happy she wouldn't be alone.

In Providence, Mom's niece Rita was at the airport to pick her up. Nancy handed her off—she had to return to Tampa on the next plane.

At first, Mom was surprised and happy to see Aranoush and her relatives, but began to spiral downward over the three-week stay. Mom was disoriented whenever she woke, not recognizing her surroundings. Several times during her stay, she would "get lost" and become frightened, saying that she was looking for someone. She ate sporadically, as she had recurring episodes of stomach upset. She wasn't used to dealing with Depends either and had a few uncomfortable moments as a result. Every day she asked whoever happened to be in the room questions about when she would be going home. I learned of some of those difficulties that had come up during Mom's stay—there were probably other unpleasant incidents about which I was never informed. It became clear to them that caring for Mom had become a bigger job than they were prepared to handle; they sent her back to Florida in three weeks, at the scheduled time.

The consensus of opinion among the relatives who interacted with Mom was that her decline was the result of being harmed by the poor care she was receiving in Florida by complete strangers. If the judge had only made the right decision at the October 2003 hearing, Mom would be fine. But, they agreed, it was the daughter, Mary, who was ultimately responsible by not supporting Lenny in his action to take charge of Mom and have her live in Rhode Island.

Aranoush's daughter, Rita, accompanied Mom back on her return flight—Nancy was there at the airport to pick her up. Mom's demeanor picked up two hundred percent when she saw Nancy. They hugged and laughed; Mom was back home.

Mom looked tired when she reached Lakeland; Lanette squeezed both her hands and hugged her. A couple of days later, she seemed to have forgotten the entire episode, chatted with Lanette as if the trip had never happened. I talked to both of them every day during that first week. While Mom sounded like she was back to her old self, Lanette noticed that her forgetfulness had become more marked. Some days, she didn't recognize the faces of friends who stopped by to visit.

Dan and I went to Lakeland for Christmas 2004. I had

been keeping up to date on Mom's health, so I wasn't too surprised when I saw that she looked weaker. We stayed at the Sheraton downtown and went back and forth to Mom's place several times each day, shopping in between. It was both funny and sad—each time I walked in, she was completely surprised to see me there.

"Hi, Mom. How are you feeling today?"

"Mary! You're here? Come and let me see you."

I sensed this could be our last Christmas together. We made a big deal about exchanging gifts: for Mom, a white crocheted cardigan and a pair of big, comfy headphones in order to better hear the TV. Her favorite gift was a chubby little photo album I'd put together. I had collected a lot of old family photos that had been forgotten, tucked away in odd places around the house. I organized them in order and filled an album that I'd found at Michael's craft store. The cover had a clear plastic panel designed to hold a photo. Rather than insert a photo in it, I made a cross-stitched rose, with my initials and date stitched in as well, and inserted that in the album cover. I knew Mom would love it. We also got some small things for Lanette that we tagged as being from Mom. Lanette was a blessing; the four of us had a cozy, bittersweet Christmas together.

Why were there no other relatives visiting Mom for the holiday? For the past couple of years, Lenny's numerous letters had given the impression that there were many people all around the country clamoring for my mother to go to Rhode Island so they could see her. Who and where were all those loving relatives he talked about?

They were: Ara and Aranoush, Mom's brother and sister in Rhode Island, Ara's children, one in Virginia and one in California, Aranoush's children, both in Rhode Island, my brother David and his son in Connecticut, and Lenny's daughter, in California. Yes, family members in four corners of the U.S., and not a single one of them ever went to Florida to visit their Auntie Elise.

Mom had lived alone for over ten years after Dad passed away—she would have been delighted to have any of them come and see her. Rather than bring her up north for a single period of a few weeks, it would have been so much better for her to have her relatives travel to Florida periodically to visit, breaking up the long stretch alone.

For years, I've tried to understand what could have been Lenny's motivation for his relentless insistence in 2004 that Mom go on that last trip. Everyone in Lakeland who knew Mom could see that she was not well enough to travel with or without an escort. Could he have been in such denial that he had become blind to her condition? Was it still all about salvaging the little money remaining to Mom?

I've learned lately that the narcissistic personality cannot accept being wrong and will go to great lengths to prove his rightness. Losing the October court hearing must have consumed Lenny. He had to prove to his supporters that it was not his fault—that the judge was wrong, and he was right. I believe that, once he got Mom to Providence that August, he had no intention of sending her back to Florida at all. He might have planned to write a letter in Mom's name, telling Barbara that she didn't want to go back to Lakeland and wished to live with her sister. Mom would graciously sign it then. Or he might dial Barbara, put Mom on the phone, and she would repeat whatever he wanted her to say. For Lenny, getting Mom to do his bidding was simple; he had manipulated much shrewder people in his career.

17

HOSPICE

O N THURSDAY, MARCH 3, 2005, I CAME HOME
from the gym to find a phone message from Barbara Keithly in Tampa: Hello, MB. I'm calling
to let you know Elise had another spell and was taken to
the hospital. They're doing tests; call me when you get this
message and I'll have more information for you.

An ice-cold knot suddenly materialized in my gut; Mom
hadn't sounded well on the phone the week before, and I
was concerned there might be something more serious going
on than just "indigestion." Lanette had been alarmed when
Mom didn't want to get out of bed the previous Sunday in
time to get ready for church. She almost never missed going
to Sunday School and church, so Lanette was sure Mom
must have been feeling worse than she admitted. I dialed
Barbara—her secretary put my call through to her. As I

feared, the news was not good.

A few years before, Mom had been diagnosed with squamous cell lung carcinoma. Since it was progressing very slowly, her doctors had decided not to treat it, reasoning that she would succumb to Alzheimer's long before the lung cancer became serious. However, after she was admitted to the hospital, an MRI showed that she had a brain tumor, which the doctors believed had metastasized from her lung to her brain.

"I'm so sorry, MB. Elise must have been in pain for some time and never said a word."

"I know, I know. She always claims she doesn't want to be a burden on anybody."

"Well, it wouldn't have changed anything had we taken her in a week earlier. The tests confirmed the tumor had been growing since her previous MRI.

". . .There's nothing they can do now?"

"She's being given pain medication, but we're talking about palliative care."

"Oh."

"I'm getting in touch with hospice. The question I need you to help decide is whether we move Elise to their care facility or set up a hospital bed in her home."

"A hospital bed in the house? They'll do that? How would that work?"

"If that's your preference, they'll bring a standard hospital bed to Elise's home, and a hospice nurse will visit her there as often as needed."

"Yes, definitely. That sounds much better than moving Mom to a strange place."

"Good, I agree. I'm glad to hear you say that."

"Have you asked Lenny what he thinks?"

"I spoke to him this afternoon. At first he wasn't sure—he asked which option was cheaper, then he must have realized that sounded crass. He said he thought the at-home option sounded better if it could be managed."

"Good."

"She'll still have Lanette there, of course, and I have an experienced person, a certified aide, whom I'll assign to relieve Lanette."

Barbara and I discussed the logistics of setting up hospice care at Mom's place. I was thankful for her level-headed guidance at the same time my head was spinning and my limbs turning to lead. I agreed to setting everything up in the living room, where there was plenty of space, rather than squeezing into the bedroom.

An hour later, Barbara called back. Lenny had found a round-trip flight from San Diego and would be in Lakeland for a few days. She recommended that we not be there at the same time. I agreed. I got on the computer and booked a flight from Newark to Tampa for Friday, March 11, when Lenny would have gone back to California.

It took a full week for the new reality to set in. I'd open my eyes each morning imagining it was all a dream until I was fully awake and had to acknowledge the fact of Mom's condition. A couple of phone calls with Lanette weren't very helpful—she was busy adjusting to the new arrangement and couldn't talk for long. My call to Dr. Hix's office didn't reveal anything new about Mom's prognosis.

On Friday, I got a cab to Newark, had a direct flight to Tampa, then rented a Hertz car for the drive to Lakeland. I-4 seemed busier than usual, but my perception could have been off because of my wish to get there in a hurry. Most of the radio stations in the area were playing country music. The repetitive tunes provided a mindless distraction from the monotony of driving: "Save A Horse" by Big and Rich, "Redneck Woman" by Gretchen Wilson.

I had a reservation at the Sheraton but decided to drive directly to Sylvester Road. There were two cars in the driveway—Lanette's and somebody else's. I eased my little compact onto the grass next to the drive and knocked instead of ringing the doorbell. Lanette opened the door, eyes pink and tired looking. We fell into each other's arms— hugged very hard.

She whispered, "Your Mom's been sleeping on and off."

We walked into the living room, the front half of which had been transformed into a hospital room. The bed stood in the center; Mom lay in it quietly, appearing to be asleep. The bed looked like those in hospitals, the mattress very high to allow easy access to the patient, with aluminum rails on the sides. One of the small tables had been placed by the bed and was covered with a variety of antiseptic-looking stuff.

I stood beside the bed, staring at Mom. A pastel blue flannel blanket covered her up to her chin. She looked so small. It took a minute for me to notice a young woman dressed in scrubs, seated across the room on a dining room chair. She'd been knitting, and she put her work down and rose. She understood that I wanted to see Mom before meeting anyone and waited courteously till I composed myself.

Lanette waited while I took in the unfamiliar scene. She nodded to the woman and grasped my hand: "Let's sit in the kitchen—I don't want to disturb her." Lanette introduced me to Jacqui. She'd been helping six hours every day, driving over from nearby Plant City. Jacqui instantly conveyed an impression of efficiency. Her speech and movements were rapid—all business—and she had a sweet smile. She turned to go back to the living room. "I'll leave you guys to talk."

Lanette and I sat opposite one another at the small island-table, twenty feet from the living room where Mom was resting.

I tried a half-hearted joke: "Lanette, you look terrible."

She sniffle-laughed, "Thanks, MB." She tugged a tissue from the dispenser, balled it up in her fist. "How was your trip?"

"Fine. I-4 wasn't too bad—the hard part was getting

out of Hoboken."

Silence.

"Is Mom going to recognize me?"

"Oh, yes. She had her meds an hour ago—she'll talk to you when she wakes up."

"OK."

"You just missed Lola, the hospice person. She's been coming in twice a day to give Elise her medication."

"Do you know what time she'll be here tomorrow?"

"She comes in the morning—she was here around nine today."

Silence fell after that.

Lanette finally asked, "Are you hungry? There's lots of leftovers in the fridge."

"Oh, no, thanks. I'm OK."

Lanette reached across the table and took my hand. She'd been through a lot the past week. She had become intensely attached to Mom and had been there with her every day, observing her decline. She told me how glad she was that I'd gotten there when I did. Mom would be happy to see me.

We talked quietly for an hour or so. Lanette mentioned the few visitors who'd stopped by. Jacqui popped her head in to let us know that Mom had awakened. She cranked up the upper half of the bed so Mom's head would be slightly raised.

I came closer: "Hi, Mom."

Mom turned her face toward me: "Mary! You're here!"

I leaned over and gave her a little peck on the cheek. "I got here a little while ago. You were having such a nice nap, I didn't want to wake you."

"Come and talk to me. I haven't seen you in such a long time."

I pulled over one of the dining room chairs and sat by the bed. It was just the right height to be at Mom's eye level.

She asked me about Dan—did he work very hard? She asked about my work—did *I* work very hard? I explained that I had retired and had lots of free time. I told her about some classes I was taking. My beading class was fun—I had learned how to do pearl knotting. Would she like me to make a necklace for her? She asked again about Dan— did he work very hard?

Pretty soon Mom's eyes started drooping—I could see she was about to doze off. I whispered to her to take a little nap, and we'd talk later.

Jacqui set her knitting aside and came over to the bed. "It's not you, it's the medication. That was a long talk for your mom—tired her out. She'll stay awake longer in the morning."

"OK. They're holding my room for me at the Sheraton. I haven't checked in yet. I'll talk to you later."

I parked behind the hotel and checked in, then used my last bit of energy to unpack. I called Dan to say good night before flopping on the king size bed.

I'd set the alarm for 6:30, giving me time to shower and have a quick breakfast before driving to Mom's at 8:00. She was wide awake when I entered her makeshift hospital room. I saw that she'd just finished a small glass of juice, and Lanette was cleaning up.

"Good morning."

Lanette said, "Hi, MB. Good timing—Elise is wide awake."

Mom turned toward me. "Mary! You're here! When did you come?"

"Hi, Mom. How are you feeling today?"

"I'm OK. Let me see you. What did you do to your hair?"

I laughed. "It came out very blond, didn't it?"

"I almost didn't recognize you. Come and talk to me."

I pulled over the same chair and sat next to the bed. Before we could do much chatting, there was a knock on the door. Lola, the hospice nurse, was a tall, strong-looking woman, probably in her fifties. We moved out of her way so she could check on Mom. I stepped farther toward the back of the room— not that Lola needed so much space, but felt a bit embarrassed. After she finished with Mom's meds, Lanette gestured me over and introduced us.

"Lola, Elise's daughter is here. She arrived yesterday. I've been telling her how her mother is in good hands."

I talked with Lola a few minutes—she did most of the

talking. She explained that Mom was not in pain, that she would be sleeping much of the time as a result of the medication, that it would be OK if I continued talking to her even when she seemed to doze off, because she would still be able to hear me.

Lola went on to tell me more about the at-home hospice arrangement. She explained it was becoming more common for families to choose this option, and it was thought to be a better choice for the patient. I thanked her; she said she'd be by again later.

"Lola, before you leave, can I ask your advice on something? See how ragged Mom's nails are? She loves to have them done at the salon, but the only time she ever goes there is when I'm around to take her. What do you think about the idea of asking one of the workers to come over and do her nails for her here?"

"I don't see why not—except, you know, she might doze off halfway through."

"Yeah, I suppose she might. But it's something she really enjoys—it could perk her up."

"Well, maybe."

By the time Lola left, Mom had fallen asleep again. Lanette said, "MB, excuse me for a minute—I have to run the washer. We only have one spare sheet for that bed."

I piped in, "One spare sheet? You must be constantly washing and drying. Can't you use any of Mom's old sheets?"

"They totally don't fit. The bed needs a special size—long twin."

"Why don't I get some new sheets? I can go over to Lakeland Square and pick up a set."

"Oh, thanks, MB—that would be a huge help."

"Since Mom's asleep, I'll run over there right now."

"Great. We'll have a snack when you get back."

My drive over and back was pretty quick as J.C. Penney only had a few choices in the extra-long twin size. I slipped in quietly; Mom was still asleep. Lanette motioned me toward the kitchen; I handed her the package.

"Thanks. We need those. I'll get them washed right away."

I was pleased that she had the good sense to launder the sheets before putting them on Mom's bed. I told Lanette my idea about getting one of the women from the salon to come over and give Mom a manicure. She thought it was an OK idea, that it wouldn't hurt to try.

Pro Top Nails at the nearby Grove Park Mall was run by Korean women, just like the salons in New Jersey and New York. I spoke to the woman in charge, explained to her my mother was not well enough to come in and that I'd like to have someone go over and give her a manicure. I was disappointed she was unable to comply with my request, citing insurance regulations.

I didn't give up on the manicure idea. I decided I would just do Mom's nails myself. I bought all the necessary stuff from the salon, including a nail buffer. Mom preferred buffing rather than polish because the shine wouldn't chip off—her nails would just gradually lose their shine.

Mom had just wakened from a nap when I got back. She looked alert, but her speech was muffled. She said something about being happy to see me. I squeezed her hand and said, "Mom, look how long your nails are. How about I trim them for you?"

Mom gazed at her hands, turned them over and back, and said, "OK." She turned her head a little to smile at me, "Thank you, *Anoushig*."

As I was filing Mom's nails, I noticed how smooth they were. A couple of them used to have ridges for as long as I could remember. The ridges were gone and all her nails were completely smooth. While I was at the last step, buffing vigorously away, Mom rested her head back on the pillow and fell asleep. I stepped back and admired my handiwork—the manicure was just as good as the pros.

Lanette was fussing in the kitchen, and Jacqui was across the room, working on her knitting. Lanette had put together a snack, and the three of us sat at the kitchen table munching away. No one said much, I'm sure out of consideration for me. It was calming just to be with them.

It was late; I was tired; we said good-bye.

Sunday morning I got to the house a few minutes before Lola arrived. She went about her routine methodically, exactly the same as the day before. I loved the way she kept talking to Mom, even while she appeared to be asleep. I asked Lola if she thought it would be all right to play some familiar tunes on the piano or sing some old songs for her. She replied that sounded like a good idea—that I should try it and see how Mom responded.

When Mom woke up, I pulled a chair up close to the bed and sat down to talk to her. We chatted about some of her friends whom I knew: told her Anita and Roger Rucker had stopped by to visit. I asked Mom if she remembered the old songs Uncle Richard used to sing.

"Of course. He loved to sing."

"Do you remember 'Silver Threads Among the Gold'?"

"Maybe. How does it go?"

"How about I play it on the piano?"

"OK."

I'd brought the sheet music with me. During the previous week, I'd gone to Colony in Manhattan and found a copy there. It was yellowed and shopworn but otherwise intact. The elderly salesman who helped me had been surprised they still had a copy; he didn't think many people remembered that good old song. It was well-known in my family, since it had been one of our uncle Richard's favorites. He was a relative on my father's side, a genuine "character," a frequent visitor in Connecticut until the '70s.

I'd read that Alzheimer's patients tend not to retain memory of recent events though are able to remember long-ago events, even from childhood. Uncle Richard's visits were experiences we shared back in the '40s and '50s, so I thought Mom would recognize his songs and be happy to hear some favorite ones he used to sing.

I sat at Mom's Clavinova and turned it on. I set the volume up a notch, since she was hard of hearing and the piano was at the far end of the room.

Darling, I am growing old,
Silver threads among the gold,
Shine upon my brow today,
Life is fading fast away.
But, my darling, you will be,
Always young and fair to me,
Yes, my darling, you will be
Always young and fair to me.

Mom stared intently at me while I played it twice through. It was hard to tell whether or not she recognized the tune.

I went back to her bedside and asked, "Mom, do you remember that song?"

She looked very hard into my eyes. "I couldn't hear it. Play it slower."

I turned up the volume another notch and played a little more slowly. I looked at her and saw that her eyes were focused on the ceiling. I was about to play it one more time, but Jacqui came over and stopped me.

"MB, would you mind not doing that any more? It's disturbing her, and she can't sleep."

"Of course I'll stop. I just thought it might revive some happy old memories."

I turned off the piano and went back to my chair next to Mom's bed. She had closed her eyes and dozed off. Oh, well—I shrugged—not all my brainy ideas are successful. I'll never know for sure, but I believe Mom recognized Uncle Richard's song and had been singing along in her mind. I don't think it was a failed experiment at all.

While she was napping, Lanette took a break and went out to run an errand. I took the opportunity to talk to Jacqui for a while. I found her to be a competent, busy woman with two children of her own and one she was in the process of adopting. She had been working in a public health care facility where she had met a teen-aged girl who had given birth to a baby boy. The girl was addicted to drugs, so the child had had health issues from the moment he was born. She felt unable to care for him and had chosen to give up the child. Jacqui had been touched by the tiny infant, a child who would have a hard time finding adoptive parents.

At the time I talked to Jacqui, she was fostering the child and going through the steps necessary to formally adopt him. I admired her and was very glad such a kind person was one of Mom's caregivers.

A couple of hours later Lanette returned, and shortly

afterwards, Lola came for her second visit. She found Mom less responsive than earlier in the day. She said something about her body slowing down, but I was too distracted to concentrate on her words. Mom's health seemed to have declined so *rapidly*. Only a few weeks before, she'd been cheerful and talkative, chatting with me on the phone.

Lanette and I sat at the dining room table, a few feet away from Mom. We gazed at her motionless figure, unaccustomed to my normally talkative mother being so still.

I thought I heard Mom make a sound; I got up and stood by the bed. Mom tossed a bit, then lay still again. Lanette said, "I think she's in for the night. Lola gave her a dose of morphine."

"Morphine. No wonder she isn't in pain."

"Lola knows what she's doing. I think she's been with hospice for a long time."

"Um-hm. I can see she's very efficient."

Lanette and Jacqui both knew more than I did about hospice procedures. They knew, for example, that once the morphine starts, the respirations will be depressed, so it is usually only a few days. I should have asked more questions.

I had become uncomfortable sitting and chatting as if Mom weren't right there, a few feet away. I said good-bye and drove back to the Sheraton. Time for a quick call to Dan at home, certain he would help me feel better. He was great at switching my attention to lighter topics, such as what take-out food he had for dinner and what our cat, Altagracia, was up to.

In bed, trying to sleep, I found the situation almost surreal. A few weeks earlier, I'd been puttering around Manhattan, taking dance and craft classes, blithely enjoying my still newly retired status. It seemed as though no time had elapsed when I found myself there in that strange room, seeing strangers all day in my Mom's upside-down home, and my sweet, energetic mother so opposite from her normal self. I took a couple of deep breaths, closed my eyes and thought, *There's simply not much within my control. All I can do is take one step at a time.*

Monday morning, I got to Mom's at 8:30. Lanette was busy straightening up the area surrounding Mom's bed. She had changed the sheets and cranked up the head of the hospital bed slightly. Despite the flurry of activity, Mom lay oblivious to it all, sound asleep.

"Good morning."

Lanette said, "Hi, MB. Elise was awake for a little while. She had a sip of water and went right back to sleep."

"I see."

"There's fresh coffee in the kitchen if you like. I'll be there in a minute."

I waited in the kitchen till she finished straightening the medication table. With coffee in hand, we kept watching for Mom to waken. She was still asleep when Lola arrived.

Lola went through her same motions, checking vital

signs and talking to Mom even though she was not awake. Moments after Lola smoothed out the flannel blanket, Mom woke up. She opened her eyes wide and looked around at us.

"What's going on?"

"It's all right, Elise. You need to rest."

"Who's there? I want to get up."

"Elise, you need to stay in bed now and get some rest."

Mom sat straight up in the bed and grabbed hold of the rails on one side. "Please, I have to get up."

Lola reached over and put an arm around Mom's shoulders, gently restraining her. I could hardly believe what was happening. Mom was actually fighting against Lola, trying to get out of bed.

I said, "Lola, can't you let her get up for a few minutes?"

"Absolutely not. We'll never get her back in bed."

For several more minutes, Lola continued to repeat her gentle but firm denials. Mom finally became tired out and allowed Lola to lay her back down. She assured me that Mom's "restless" behavior was to be expected. She stayed by Mom's side, continuing to talk quietly while holding her hand. I watched as Lola gave Mom a heavy dose of morphine. She didn't leave until Mom was sound asleep.

When Lola returned later for her second visit, she could see that I was still upset. She spoke to me privately, explaining that Mom could still hear, even while she appeared to be unconscious. She suggested it might be calming for Mom to hear me talk quietly to her and tell her reassuring things about anything that might be worrying her. I thanked her; she said she would see us in the morning.

Tuesday morning, Jacqui came in early and was helping Lanette straighten up around the bed when I got there. When Lola arrived, she followed the identical procedure with Mom. Mom slept soundly through all our comings and goings.

Lola gave some added instructions to Jacqui and Lanette before saying goodbye. I looked at the two women, trying to read their faces. They both retreated to the far side of the room, allowing me a little privacy with Mom.

I sat down by her bed and began to talk softly, close to her ear. It felt strange at first, but I grew more at ease as I went on about whatever came to mind. I told her about some changes I'd made to my house in Hoboken, told her about an Armenian dish I'd made for Dan and how much he liked it. I paused and then got to the hard part—I talked to her about Lenny and David. I told Mom they were both doing well and she didn't need to worry about either of them. I went on about how the three of us sometimes had disagreements, but we had apologized and were friends again. I said that David missed her and wanted her to know that he was doing much better, that she didn't need to worry about him anymore.

Very softly, I sang a couple verses of an Armenian hymn

that Mom loved. It was actually the only Armenian hymn I knew the words to—I surprised myself that I still remembered it. I recall clearly when, more than fifty years ago, Mom's mother used to visit us in Connecticut. She was always singing Armenian hymns as she puttered around the house, and this one she sang most often. I knew the hymn in Armenian only. It may exist in English, though I've never heard it.

Mom lay still, not seeming to respond to me at all other than through slight changes in her breathing pattern. This one-way conversation went on for at least an hour. I was running low on topics; Jacqui came over and touched my shoulder—it was time to stop.

"Why don't you go out a little while for some fresh air?"

"OK."

I leaned over the bed rail to give Mom a tiny peck on the forehead. Her skin was amazing—she had hardly a line in her face. The pale blue of the blanket folded beneath her chin was a good color for her. Was it my imagination? I think she looked more peaceful after my chatter. I picked up my car keys and told Lanette and Jacqui, "See you later."

I ought to have read their faces at that moment; I would have understood why they felt I should go out for a while. They knew I didn't want to be there when Mom breathed her last.

I drove around the parts of Lakeland that I knew. Then

I ventured into some parts that I didn't know and got lost. I eventually found my way again and stopped by a lake to watch the swans. I drove back to Sylvester Road.

The bed was gone. Jacqui said, "It's a good thing you weren't here to see how they took her body away."

18

TWO FUNERALS

I COULD NEVER HAVE FUNCTIONED over the next few days without Lanette—she stayed by me, doing her best to keep me focused. The most unpleasant job I had before me was choosing a casket. Heath Funeral Home had two separate roomfuls from which to choose. The first had the basic, no-frills caskets. Customers who were interested in better ones were directed to the second room.

As Lanette and I entered the mildly perfumed second room, a chill ran through me as I surveyed the gleaming display there. The caskets were spaced discreetly apart, each one highly polished and bearing ornate hardware. No price tags, of course. We managed to temporarily shed the salesperson by claiming to be sisters who wished to browse alone. We narrowed down our possible choices to two that were nicely designed without being ostentatious. The salesman rejoined us and, with his assistance, we agreed on the casket for my mother.

We gave him the address of Lakeside Baptist—they would handle everything from that point. All we had to do is be at Lakeside on time for the memorial service the next day. Heath would also take care of transporting the casket to the airport in Bridgeport, Connecticut, on Friday.

Mom's friend Anita helped me make the arrangements at Lakeside and suggested that Kermis Frost would be a good person to conduct the service. Kermis was a member of Lakeside and a retired pastor. Mom had been fond of him and his wife, Jean, their home just a few houses away on Sylvester. Lakeside's pastor of many years, Craig Sherouse, had recently moved on to a church in Georgia; the new pastor, Dean Rucker, had been at Lakeside for only a short time, and Mom had barely known him. Kermis was the perfect person to conduct the memorial service for Mom—he was pleased I asked him to do it.

Once I talked to Anita, she started the chain of phone calls to inform all those who had known my mother. Betsy Cable agreed to sing two of Mom's favorite hymns. Dee Grandbois, the church's chef, would cater the post-service reception in the church dining room.

On March 17, 2005, every seat in the chapel at Lakeside Baptist was filled; my mother was so loved by everyone in the congregation. I noticed there were a few attendees who were not from the church, such as Pixie and Fred Coleman. I knew they were fond of my mother—it was a pity they had been drawn into my brother Lenny's courtroom drama two years earlier. They didn't speak to me.

Conspicuously absent was Sherry Baker. I'm sure she'd been genuinely fond of Mom—I think she was just embarrassed to see me after her collusion with Lenny.

Good friends sat by me in the front row: Anita and Roger Rucker on my right, Nancy Bigam and Lanette Dees on my left. Just as Kermis had risen to begin the service, Lanette reached across Nancy and tapped my hand. She wanted to sit next to me. I looked at Nancy to see if that was OK with her; she quickly moved, changing seats. Lanette then sat right next to me and squeezed my hand for the entire service. She was going to have a difficult adjustment learning to get along without Mom.

Kermis first read the obituary I had written for the *Lakeland Ledger*, then added his own comments based on his personal friendship with Mom. Betsy Cable's solo was next—she sang "In the Garden," Mom's favorite hymn.

At that same moment, in a college town halfway across the country, Betsy's daughter, Bethany, was writing about my mom. It was a beautifully written tribute that included a description of the hard life Mom experienced before coming to the U.S. She wrote how Mom loved everyone, that there was a light about her, and how no one could ever be angry or sad or upset in her presence. She described how her heart had broken when she and her mother visited my mom in the hospital. Bethany said she knew Mom's memorial service was being held that very day and how much she wished she could be there. She ended her "Anniverse" blog entry:

Mrs. Yakoubian, the world was a better, brighter place with you in it. Not Alzheimer's, not even cancer could rob you of the light God gave you. When you couldn't hold it any longer, you passed it on to us. We will carry His light here for you for a little while, long enough to pass it on to whom we can. I don't think mine will ever be as bright as yours, but that isn't saying much.

Kermis' message, and the rest of the service, went by in a blur. Betsy sang "Depart in Peace" in closing. I turned and hugged Lanette for I'm not sure how many minutes, so I wouldn't have to watch the pallbearers close the casket.

Several people stopped afterwards to offer their condolences and talk to me about their fond remembrances of my mother. It touched me once again to see how loved she was by all who knew her. Everyone then filed a few yards down the covered walkway to the dining room, where Dee had a hot and cold buffet laid out. I used the time there to talk to friends; I couldn't manage to eat anything.

After I'd said goodbye to the last group of people, Lanette and I drove to the house to have a few minutes alone; we needed to plan for our trip the next day. I felt indebted to Lanette for all she'd done caring for my mother. Her attention had been over and above that of simply a caregiver. I couldn't imagine saying goodbye to her and traveling back home alone the day after the memorial service. Dan and I decided to bring Lanette to Connecticut for Mom's funeral there. I told her it would mean a lot to me if she would agree to go to Stratford with me and attend the service with us.

Our agenda was to go first to Hoboken, where Lanette would stay at our home Friday and Saturday night. On Sunday, the three of us would drive to Stratford, where we had booked rooms at a local hotel for two nights, then return to New Jersey on Tuesday, March 22. Lanette's return flight to Tampa was on Tuesday evening.

I talked to my cousin Bob Yakoubian, who took over as my Connecticut lifeline, making all the necessary arrangements. He lived in Stratford and knew which funeral home to use, which church to schedule the service in, and where to book the post- funeral dinner. He promised to handle every detail.

Dan met Lanette and me at Newark Airport with a taxi for the ride to Hoboken. It was all a new experience for Lanette—she kept a brave face, but I guessed she was probably ill at ease. Dan and I decided to take her around Manhattan the next day. She'd never been to New York before, and sightseeing would help keep us both from brooding.

It turned out to be a good day for our side trip. We pretended to be tourists with her, going on the Grayline Hop-On Hop-Off sightseeing bus. We'd made arrangements to later meet a couple of friends for dinner at the Rodeo Bar, one of the few places in Manhattan where you could hear country music. Lanette had perked up by the end of the day.

Sunday morning March 20, we headed for Stratford. I had with me a rough draft of my eulogy and spent much of the one-hour drive working on it. It was shortly after noon when we checked into the hotel. Stratford had grown since I lived there as a kid—there hadn't been any hotels at all back then.

Bob and Maryanne had invited us over for brunch. We stayed there through the evening—Bob and I went over the logistics of the funeral for the following day. There would be a viewing in the morning and then a service at Stratford Baptist Church, right across the street from Adzima Funeral Home. Lenny and I had agreed, a few days earlier, to limit our eulogy comments to a maximum of fifteen minutes each; I had mine timed at ten.

Monday morning, the three of us met Bob at Adzima, then crossed over together to the church. The service was scheduled to start at 12:00 noon. At 11:30 Lenny showed up along with our cousin Rita, very agitated, saying the service had to be delayed till 1:00. He said that numerous people were on the way from Rhode Island, and that we had to wait for them. All right—I agreed to the delay.

We sat in a pew and waited. Lenny sat on the left side of the church with Rita, her mother Aranoush, and Uncle Ara. Behind them was another cousin, Gail, and members of her family, all from Rhode Island. I sat on the right side with Dan and Lanette. Bob and his family sat in the row behind me, along with cousins JoAnne and Thom, Bob's sister and brother. Several family friends who still lived in the Stratford area arrived in twos and threes. By 12:00, there were approximately sixty people seated in the pews.

We continued to wait. Pretty soon, some began whispering, probably questioning why the service had not yet begun. By 12:30, a few people who didn't want to wait any longer quietly slipped out. Bob slid over by my side and whispered that we ought to start as no one else from Rhode Island had shown up. It was already half an hour past the originally scheduled time. I replied that I had promised Lenny we would delay—perhaps we could wait another ten minutes and then begin. He nodded and said OK.

At 12:45, no one else had appeared, though a few more people had tiptoed out; I signaled Pastor Genewicz to begin the service. Following a few minutes of gentle organ music, he stepped to the pulpit and began with the Call to Worship and prayer. Following a congregational hymn and scripture reading, it was time for Lenny and me to each deliver a eulogy. Pastor Genewicz introduced me first.

The instant I stepped up to the pulpit, the weight of the moment fully struck me. It took me a minute or two to regain my composure; the group I was facing remained a blur—I couldn't focus clearly on anyone seated there in the church. This is what I said about my mother that day, March 21, 2005, at our hometown funeral service:

When my mother, Elise Yakoubian, came into a room, it was like sunshine instantly brightening a cloudy day. My mother was a true Christian, whose positive attitude toward life brought joy to everyone around her. I believe all of us here today know this. So let's celebrate my mother's life together and let's try to keep a little of her positive outlook in our hearts always.

My mother taught me so much over the years; I'd like to share with you today a few of those memories. One of my earliest and fondest memories was when my late brother Johnny and I were little children. A favorite time of ours took place while Mom was ironing. In those days, sheets were made only out of cotton—polyester hadn't been invented yet—and they came out of the wash pretty wrinkled. Of course, my mother would never put wrinkled sheets on our beds, so once a week was ironing day. Mom would take down the ironing board out of its wall cabinet and spread old sheets underneath it on the floor. Johnny and I would then sit ourselves down at the edge and listen to her tell us Bible stories.

Mom was a great story-teller, always including lots of colorful details. Sometimes she let us choose which story we wanted to hear—we'd take turns choosing. I recall Johnny's favorite was about Joseph and his coat of many colors.

I'll always cherish the memory of those story-telling days and of the many other things my mother taught me— how to sew my own clothes, how to make the tastiest apple pies—but whatever it was, she always taught me to strive to do my best at it.

After my parents moved to Lakeland, it became difficult to visit them as often. But we'd talk on the phone, and I was glad to hear how happy they were in their new sur- roundings. The happiest 27 years of my mother's life were there, among her dear friends at Lakeside Baptist Church. It's a comfort to me to know she was able to fulfill her wish to die in her home there, near her cherished friends.

It's been a special comfort for me to know that during the final eight months of her life, she was cared for by a most dedicated and loving caregiver. Lanette Dees is here today, and I hope you will take the time to talk to her be- fore you go home. Lanette will tell you of the immediate and breathtaking bond that formed between them. Lanette feels that what my mother gave to her was even more valu- able than the care and attention she was able to give to my mother. She tells me that my mother taught her lessons in life that have changed her forever. I am envious of Lanette for that precious time she spent caring for my mother dur- ing the final months of her life.

I was fortunate to be there with my mother during her last week, and I'd like to share with you my last words to her. In the morning on March 15, Mom's hospice nurse came to the house. Lola was a gentle person, with a calming, musical voice. While she was standing next to Mom (who by that time appeared to be in a coma), she leaned over and talked quietly right next to her ear. I was taken aback as I believed that Mom was no longer able to hear anyone talk. After Lola said goodbye to my mother, she explained to me that Mom most likely could hear us and could very well be holding on, waiting for her children to assure her that we would be all right.

That afternoon, I talked to Mom, very close to her ear. I told her I wanted to sing her favorite hymn to her, the hymn which her own mother used to sing so often. Close to her ear, I sang that Armenian hymn, and then I told Mom that her three children loved her very much and that we would be OK. I told her she didn't have to worry about us any more and she could close her eyes and rest.

A little later I left. One hour later, while Lanette held her ear to my mother's heart, she stopped breathing.

When I sat back in my pew, Lanette grabbed my hand and squeezed and squeezed. Pastor Genewicz then invited Lenny to deliver his eulogy. He stepped behind the pulpit and stood there for a moment, grinning, then said, "Well, as usual for me, I'm unprepared."

What? He's got to be kidding! I stared at him grinning away up there, and said to myself, "No, he couldn't really be unprepared."

Lenny went on to excuse his lack of preparation to time constraints, and asked his audience to bear with him as he would do what he could to "wing it." He began by describing his childhood years in Stratford, recalling how much fun he used to have playing with Cousin Thom in the woods behind Stonybrook Mall. His comments then evolved into reminiscences of later exploits with school friends, and a description of his affection for some of his favorite spots in town, such as the Shakespeare Festival grounds. After thirty minutes, Bob leaned over and whispered, "When is he going to end?"

I rolled my eyes and shrugged. Not done yet, Lenny continued in the same vein for another ten minutes. Bob finally took action: He glared at Lenny and, with the side of his hand, began to make slicing motions across his neck. Lenny got the message. He assured his audience he could go on telling more stories, but his time was up. He stepped down from the pulpit after saying not one word about Mom.

The discomfort he had created was quickly dispelled by Sharon Thompson's beautiful rendition of "In the Garden." Then came a brief Meditation and another alteration in the program.

When I agreed to delaying the start time, I'd also agreed

to a second change, said OK to adding one hymn during which Cousin Gail from Rhode Island, an experienced organist, would accompany the singing. Lenny felt it was essential to include singing the Lord's Prayer in Armenian. So Gail played and the lone voice of Aranoush could be heard intoning the Armenian words. I don't think anyone else knew it; I certainly didn't.

The service ended with a Benediction. When the pall-bearers stepped forward to close the lid of the casket, I feigned coughing into a tissue so I could turn my head and look away.

Outside the church stood the hearse and a line of black cars waiting to take us to Lakeview Cemetery. Just as Dan and I were about to leave the church, Lenny came rushing over. He demanded that I ask the funeral director to open the casket so he could remove Mom's gold chain and engagement ring. I have no idea what the protocol is when it comes to jewelry; my automatic response was, "No way." We both had many souvenirs by which to remember Mom, it wasn't necessary to remove her jewelry. Lenny was furious, but I refused to discuss it further.

The funeral procession snaked through Stratford and into Bridgeport, circling around then rolling slowly through the twin stone pillars flanking the entrance to Lakeview Cemetery. Dan and I were directed to sit on folding chairs by the newly dug grave at the Yakoubian family plot. On headstones visible nearby, we silently read the names engraved on them: John and Mary, my paternal grandparents; Leon, my father; George, his brother; and John, my baby brother. Most of the others in attendance remained standing for the brief graveside ceremony.

Back to the black cars, we left the cemetery and headed for the next and final gathering of the day—the meal at Liedle's Restaurant in Stratford.

They had cordoned off half the restaurant and set up several round tables for us. Pastor Genewicz sat at a table with my little group: Dan, Lanette, Bob, and Maryanne. I found him to be a talkative, entertaining person. We chatted about the old days in Stratford when our parents were living. I learned that the remaining members of the old Alliance Church we used to attend had gravitated to Stratford Baptist as their new home church. The Rhode Island relatives, along with Lenny and David, were seated at other tables; none of them talked to us.

I hadn't had anything to eat all day—I should have had a little something, but the events of the day had affected me more than I was willing to admit. We had just laid to rest my sweet mother, someone who was dearly loved by every person seated at those big round tables, munching and chatting away.

Time to leave. Dan, Lanette, and I began walking past the row of tables toward the exit. Halfway there I observed what looked like a political gathering going on next to one of the tables. Lenny was standing on a chair, addressing his crowd of followers. The entire group of relatives from Rhode Island were standing around his makeshift podium, listening intently to whatever words of wisdom he was imparting. I should have stopped to hear what he was saying, but I didn't. I was nauseated; he had no sense of decency. We drove back to the hotel, from which we would be returning to New Jersey the next morning.

The next day, our drive back to Hoboken took place practically in silence. I went zombielike through the motions of unpacking, saying good-bye to Lanette, and sending her off in a taxi to the airport.

Lanette still had work to do when she returned to Lakeland. She and Barbara would sort through the house, pack up a few mementos for Lenny, David, and me, and get the place ready to sell. The inheritance check Barbara would send Lenny would not be for the $90,000 he might once have received, but for $2,830.93. Per my request, they would deliver the Clavinova to Kermis and Jean Frost.

I still had a few clerical things to take care of: a letter and gift to Lanette, and thank-you notes to those who had sent flowers, made donations to Lakeside, or taken part in either of the two funerals. I sent a thank-you note to those in Rhode Island as well, even though they made donations to their own church there rather than to Mom's church in Florida. Finally, I wrote a note to include with my donation, though I knew it could never be adequate thanks for the many years of happiness the people of Lakeside Baptist lovingly provided my mom.

Suddenly I was without a mother. She was not going to be there to answer the phone any more. No matter when I called, she was cheerful, happy to hear from me, interested in whatever I was up to. I knew I'd never be able to get used to being without her.

19

POSTLUDE

I N 2019, AFTER YEARS OF CONSIDERING the idea, I decided to write the story of my mother's last years. Once I started on the project, I found myself reliving experiences that had happened fifteen years earlier, entire conversations coming back to mind. I was also fortunate to have internet access to the Polk County Court Records. Every legal action, and every communication concerning my mother as of 2001, was available for download. The 1,177 pages of court documents in probate case #2000CP0018140000XX filled four large binders on my bookshelf.

I decided that my recollections would be sharper if I were to visit the people and places where the events of my story took place. Over the years, Anita Rucker was the only person in Lakeland with whom I'd kept in touch. She had moved to Azalea Park, a continuing care community, after her husband passed away. I heard from her about how theological differences that had been simmering among Lakeside Baptist church members had grown till the congregation split in two. Then more members switched to other churches, till it completely fell apart. It came as a shock when I learned that, in 2016, Lakeside Baptist had closed permanently. I was thankful at least that my mother never witnessed what happened to her beloved church.

Another shocker was learning of the death of Lanette Dees. Her mother, Sharon Dees, explained to me how Lanette had been taking prescription medications and accidentally overdosed on a lethal combination of meds and alcohol. Nine years after Lanette's passing, Sharon continues to grieve for her sweet daughter. Lanette was forty-three when she died.

News that wasn't very shocking was the fate of Mark Dolly, my pennysaver lawyer. Multiple complaints had been filed with the Florida Bar against him, two of those complaints culminating in disciplinary action, at which time his license to practive law was suspended. Looking back, my first and biggest mistake had been hiring that inept attorney. I'm convinced that, had I hired Scott Langston initially, he wouldn't have advised me to go the guardian route.

I told Anita about my return-to-Lakeland idea. She was happy to hear we'd see each other again and suggested I stay at the Hampton Inn in Lakeside Village, a new mall close to Azalea Park. Dan and I settled on the first week in

October 2019 for our Lakeland adventure.

I went ahead and got in touch with everyone I was able to find and scheduled appointments to visit each person. I had in my possession the perfect ice breaker for when I got together with Mom's friends after such a long period of time: photographs! I had put together a fat album of photos taken at Mom's ninetieth birthday party, and actually had the foresight to label each photo with people's names. It was like looking at a Lakeside Baptist Reunion party. I also had a smaller album of photos from Mom's ninety-first birthday party, but that one had no IDs included, so it was up to whoever was thumbing through to identify those in the photos.

On October 1, Dan and I boarded our flight to Tampa; an Uber car delivered us from the airport to our hotel in Lakeland. We were so organized—we had scheduled two meetings per day on each of the seven days we'd be there. In addition to seeing Anita, we had lunch or dinner dates with Mom's friends: Linda Thomas, Betsy Cable, Charlotte Markham, Sherry Baker, and my attorney, Scott Langston.

One afternoon, we stopped by Florida Presbyterian to look again at what might have been. It was all as attractive as I'd remembered, complete with egrets strutting at the edge of Lake Hunter.

Another day we went out to Bartow to re-visit the ninth floor of the Polk County Courthouse. The blue elevator doors there opened onto a silent, empty floor, nothing in session. We peeked in through the tiny square of glass in the door to the courtroom where our hearing had been held—it seemed smaller than I remembered. In the waiting area along the hallway, Dan showed me the row of chairs where he'd sat and waited the entire time the hearing was going on. We both sat there for a minute, mutely recalling the last time we'd been in that building fifteen years earlier.

The saddest day was when we met with Sharon Dees, Lanette's mother. She was a realtor and had bought Mom's house on Sylvester Road. The house was between tenants, unoccupied when we were there, so she took us to see it.

Outside, the front yard was completely overgrown, weeds knee high and the old flower bed neglected and barren. The single plant that had managed to flourish was the rubber plant, grown to twenty feet in height.

We followed Sharon in through the foyer into the living room. It was dark, damp, dusty. We trailed through each room, and then out to the back. The once lush lanai was as dead as the rest of the house—not a shred of green to be seen. The entire house exuded sadness; it was an empty shell. Seeing Mom's house in that state was painful. I couldn't shake the feeling of transience—not a trace of the busy life that had once existed there.

Anita had told me that many of the former Lakeside people had switched to The Rock community church. The Rock had been founded by Monty and Kim Davis, who used to be music directors at Lakeside Baptist. I decided to go there on Sunday and perhaps see some familiar faces. I did find quite a few, including Frances Robson, one of Mom's Sunday School classmates, and Dr. Abbott, Mom's dentist. We took photos together and got big hugs all around. It was a happy experience to find old friends after so many years.

On our last day in Florida, we had arranged to leave for Tampa early so we'd have time to see Barbara Keithly, Mom's guardian, before catching our flight home. Barbara ran Magnolia Manor, an assisted living facility in Lutz, Florida, twenty minutes north of Tampa. She had invited her assistant, Nancy Bigam, to join us as well. The four of us sat at a table in Magnolia's front lounge and had fun looking through Mom's photo album and recalling stories from fifteen years earlier.

Barbara said something to me that I'll always remember: "Of all the guardianship posts I've held over the years, you're the only one who has ever come back." Thank you, Barbara.

Her recollections of Lenny all included his focus on money. She admitted that his continual harassment nearly caused her to resign, but she was so fond of Mom, she stayed on for her sake. Barbara's bottom line after Mom's case was settled: "Some things are worth fighting for."

My return to Lakeland adventure was a rewarding one. If I were to encapsulate everyone's comments about Mom into one, it would be: "She believed in goodness, looked for the good in people, and listened."

About the Author

Mary Beth Yakoubian teaches dance and fitness; *There's Nothing Wrong With Her* is her first book-length work.

After ten years of writing short stories, her current work recalls the sometimes humorous and often sad anecdotes that chronicle her mother's inexorable decline with Alzheimer's disease.

In addition to earning graduate degrees at New York University and Hunter College, she honed her writing skills at the acclaimed Gotham Writers Workshop in Manhattan.

Born and raised in Stratford, Connecticut, M.B. moved to New York City at twenty, where she worked as a high school teacher and later met her husband, Dan Cox, of Philadelphia. The couple chose to become commuters, settling in trendy Hoboken, New Jersey, where they currently live along with their cats, Solo and Vader.

She and her husband spend their spare time going to the opera, theater, and bluegrass concerts.

CPSIA information can be obtained
at www.ICGtesting.com
Printed in the USA
BVHW031000130821
613494BV00003B/6

9 780578 886473